MERSEYSIDE MURDERS OF THE 1920S

Merseyside Murders
of the 1920s

by David Parry

Merseyside Murders of the 1920s

First published in 2007
by Palatine Books,
Carnegie House,
Chatsworth Road
Lancaster LA1 4SL
www.palatinebooks.com

British Library Cataloguing-in-Publication data
A catalogue record for this book is available from the British Library

ISBN 13: 978-1-874181-43-9

Designed and typeset by Carnegie Book Production
Drawings by Ivan Frontani
www.carnegiebookproduction.com

Printed and bound in the UK by Alden Press

Contents

Acknowledgements

The author wishes to thank the staff of the Liverpool Record Office for their help during the research for this book. Particular thanks is expressed to Ivan Frontani who provided the line drawings and to Janet McLarney who supplied the background highlights within the text. Thank you also to all those at Carnegie Book Production who assisted in the preparation of the manuscript for publication.

No More Money

The watercourse known as the River Alt flows from Huyton, northwest-wards through Croxteth Park, past Aintree, Maghull and Sefton. Then near Formby it swings eastwards, and finally southwards to enter Liverpool bay at Hightown. An area of land to the south of Formby takes its name from the river and is known as Little Altcar. Our first story, which is centred here, begins in Formby on the evening of Sunday 21 March 1920.

The public bar of the Blundell Arms Hotel opened for business that evening at the usual time of 7 p.m. One of the first customers was a local man, a labourer called James Clayton who worked in the Liverpool docks. Clayton, who was alone, bought a pint of beer at the bar and settled himself at a corner table. From here he had a good view of the room, and of the bar which ran along one side. Contentedly, Clayton sipped his beer, little knowing how eventful the evening would prove to be.

As the room began to fill up with its Sunday night customers, James Clayton gazed over to the bar. A man in a rather crumpled grey suit was ordering a whisky and soda. As Clayton watched, the man became involved in some kind of disagreement. He was accusing the barman of staring at him. After a brief exchange of words, the grey-suited man, who had a distinctive military bearing, said to the barman: 'You are only one man, and not a very big one at that'. The argument was soon over and the man sat down across the room from Clayton.

An hour passed. The room became busier and filled with tobacco smoke. From his position near the door, James Clayton noticed that the grey-suited man kept pulling a dark metallic object out of his side jacket pocket and then putting it back again. As Clayton watched, he realised the object was a handgun.

In 1920 guns circulated quite freely. Clayton had often seen men trading them in the docks. The Great War had ended only recently, flooding the country with illegally held souvenirs of that terrible conflict. Nevertheless, seeing a firearm being handled in such a cavalier fashion made Clayton feel distinctly uneasy.

At 10 p.m. the bell rang for closing time and customers made their way into the cool night air. Some were chatting and saying their farewells as Clayton came out of the hotel and stood for a moment to prepare himself for his walk home. Then, a yard or two away, the man in the grey suit suddenly staggered and collapsed to his knees on the pathway, before falling forward on his face. Clayton picked the man up and, taking him to a nearby lamp, told him to wipe his nose, which had begun to bleed profusely. The man put a hand into a pocket and brought out a revolver.

Before Clayton could react to this threat, the man said to him: 'I have put four bullets into my wife'. Clayton, while disbelieving this statement, snatched the revolver from the man, who then ran round the corner of the hotel. Clayton, by now incensed by the drunken man's outrageous behaviour, followed him around the corner, jumped on his back and, after the man had again collapsed to the ground, held him down firmly.

Soon afterwards, a police van pulled up. The man was arrested and Clayton went into the van as well. At Formby police station, Clayton handed the revolver to Inspector King. It had its five chambers fully loaded with cartridges. The hammer of the weapon had been drawn back. A box of 36 cartridges was also found in the grey suit, together with a lady's gold watch, a gold guard and a locket, and just over three pounds in cash. The drunken and stupefied man was put into a cell for the night on a charge of being drunk and disorderly.

At 7 a.m. the next morning, Sergeant Kenyon went into the drunken man's cell and asked him for his name and address. The man gave the name Herbert Edward Rawson Salisbury. He would not tell Kenyon his address. The sergeant then asked, 'Where does your wife live?', to which Salisbury immediately replied, 'My wife is lying dead on the river bank, past Tommy Rimmer's on the main road. I shot her last night.'

Salisbury's statement came as a complete surprise to Kenyon because James Clayton had not told anyone about what Salisbury had said to him the previous night. A police search party was sent out along the Liverpool Road and, at the foot of the embankment of the River Alt, about a mile from the Blundell Arms, was found the body of a woman, her face covered in dried blood. She had four bullet wounds in the right temple. Out of sight from the road, the body was in such a position that it might well have lain undiscovered for days or weeks. In a leather handbag near the woman's body were some copper coins and two half crowns.

At Formby police station, Salisbury asked Inspector King: 'Have you found the lady?' When told that the woman was dead, Salisbury was alleged to have added: 'Thank God for that. We agreed to end our lives together when the money was done. We had £700 and the money I had on me was all we had left'.

It had begun to look as if after Salisbury had killed the woman, took drink to give himself enough nerve to shoot himself, and then drank so much that he was unable to complete his part of a suicide pact.

On the Tuesday morning, Salisbury appeared at Formby Police Court on a charge of wilful murder. He was remanded in custody for seven days. The dead woman was not Salisbury's wife; the couple had been living together. She was Mrs Alice Pearson, aged 38, a native of Leeds and the divorced wife of a Leeds railway goods clerk called Mark William Pearson.

Nowadays it is usual for a brief inquest to be opened only for evidence of identification to be heard. The rest of the inquest is usually postponed until any criminal proceedings have been completed. However, in 1920 a full inquest was heard by a coroner, after which a jury was then expected to return its verdict as to the cause of death. Consequently, an inquest into Mrs Pearson's death was begun in the Formby Police Court immediately after Salisbury had been remanded. Coroner Brighouse presided.

Salisbury had worked as a headwaiter. He had served during the war as a driver in the Machine Gun Corps of the American Army, and he told Sergeant Kenyon that he had married in East Boston, USA. He had also said he had a son who would now be 11 years old. Salisbury left his wife and son in Rhode Island early in 1916 and had not seen or heard from them since. Aged 33, he was a native of Formby and had been taken to the United States in 1900.

Opening the inquest at Formby on 23 March, Mr Brighouse said:

It would appear that the deceased was a divorced woman and that her husband had obtained a decree nisi, although it is not quite certain whether that decree had been made absolute. He obtained it against her in consequence of her misconduct with Salisbury. The two had been cohabiting at the house of Mrs Stocker at 17 Castle Street, Southport, and on the 21st of this month they came to Formby, evidently with the intention of dying together. Salisbury seems to have shot Mrs Pearson, four bullets having been found in her head, and then failed to carry out the contract. In order to get himself up to the point of doing so, he took some drink, but he took more, I suppose, than he anticipated and eventually got into such as state that he recollected neither whether he had killed her nor what he had to do to himself.

Dennis Rhodes, a company secretary from Stockport, said that Alice Pearson was his sister-in-law whom he had last seen at Liverpool on 28 March 1919. She married Mark Pearson in 1910 and there were no children. Until about 1916 the Pearsons lived in the Meanwood district of Leeds. In 1917 the husband was conscripted into the army. About the beginning of March 1919, while her husband was still in the forces, Alice's family found out that she had met Herbert Salisbury and had left Leeds.

The Rhodes family told the Leeds police that Alice was missing. The police traced her to a house at 83 Queens Road, off Breck Road, in Liverpool. She was living there with Salisbury, posing as his wife. Surprisingly as it may now seem, the Leeds police took Alice back to Yorkshire, and delivered her up to her parents at Vernon Road in the city. Mr Pearson was sent for and was told of Alice's relationship with Salisbury. Gallantly, he undertook to forgive her and offered to take her back.

Alice Pearson would have none of this. She declined her husband's offer of a proverbial olive branch and two or three days later, she left Leeds again, saying she was determined to rejoin her lover in Liverpool. According to Dennis Rhodes, he wrote to his sister-in-law at Queens Road, asking her to meet him. This she did and she told him that she was perfectly happy. Salisbury told Rhodes that he hoped Mr Pearson would take divorce proceedings against Alice without delay, so that they could be legally married.

Herbert Salisbury had seemingly told that police that he and Alice Pearson had at one time possessed £700. Part of this sum may have belonged to Salisbury, because Mr Rhodes testified that when Alice left Leeds she took £500 with her. Apparently, the cash had gradually dwindled down to almost nothing in the twelve-month period up to the shooting.

At the inquest, the evidence of Dr Carter, the police surgeon, was read out by Coroner Brighouse, Externally, Dr Carter had found upon the body of Alice Pearson, four wounds in the region of the right temple, with singeing of the surrounding skin. At the base of the left side of the head was a lacerated wound with brains protruding. Internally, reported Dr Carter, there was a multiple fracture of the base of the skull. This had caused severe haemorrhage and death. Two bullets were found within the head.

On Wednesday 7 April at Formby, Salisbury pleaded guilty to a charge of murder and was committed to stand trial by jury at the Liverpool Spring Assizes. The assizes were due to open the following week. At this committal hearing, as was usual, Salisbury's solicitor did not call any witnesses for the defence, reserving them for the trial itself. Salisbury's guilty plea was unusual, but it was consistent with his almost unbearable feelings of remorse.

The trial of Herbert Salisbury for the murder of Alice Pearson opened on Thursday 22 April 1920 before Mr Justice McCardie and a jury at St George's Hall, Liverpool. Salisbury entered the dock in fine style, his suit freshly ironed. His military bearing, which James Clayton had noticed in the bar of the Blundell Arms, was clearly evident. Salisbury looked round the court with a cool, almost challenging gaze. When asked by the Clerk of the Assize to plead to the murder charge, Salisbury, in a firm voice, replied: 'Guilty'. A moment of silence followed this dramatic statement.

Mr Justice McCardie, having anticipated such a plea, said:

> In this case I shall direct that a plea of not guilty be entered. I deem it desirable that the case should be established against the person charged, in open court, so that all the facts connected with the crime may be before the court. The prisoner has the advantage of being represented by Mr Madden.

Salisbury did not seem to be much concerned with the preliminary formalities, but he followed with intermittent interest the opening address of prosecuting counsel A. J. Ashton KC and the evidence which was presented after it.

In his opening remarks to the jury, the prosecuting counsel mentioned Salisbury's departure from England to America some twenty years before, his return to England during the war, and his military service in France, where he suffered from trench fever and was also wounded. In September 1918, Salisbury became a patient at a Leeds hospital. There, he met Alice Pearson, whose husband Mark was a soldier and former clerk with the London and North Western Railway Company. Because of Alice's adultery with Salisbury, Mark obtained a decree nisi in June 1919. This was made absolute early in 1920.

Mrs Pearson had withdrawn several of her own investments, the money from which had enabled her and Salisbury to travel up and down the country. They stayed in Mrs Stocker's house in Southport from 20 March, living, according to Mr Ashton, 'a sober, quiet and respectable life'. They used the names 'Mr and Mrs Rawson'. The couple left Southport on the day of the shooting. That afternoon, they were seen near the Royal Hotel in Formby, walking in the direction of Liverpool.

After the evidence for the prosecution had been given, including as it did the alleged admission from Salisbury that he had planned the killing, it was abundantly clear that a guilty verdict would be returned in due course. Were Salisbury to be found guilty of murder, the only sentence that the judge could pass would be death by hanging. In an effort to save his client from the gallows, the best option available to defence counsel Mr Madden was to try to convince the jury that, at the time of the killing at least, Salisbury was insane.

As the law stood in 1920, the burden of proof of insanity rested upon the defence. It was a matter of convincing the jury of two things. The first was that at the time of committing the murderous act, the accused did not know that what he was doing was wrong. Secondly, the jury had to believe that the killer was, through mental disease, unable to understand the nature and quality of his actions when committing the murder. The prosecution did not have to prove that the killer was sane, but they could call evidence to that effect. The rather paradoxical verdict of 'guilty but insane' might then be returned.

Mr Madden called two medical experts, both of whom said that Salisbury suffered from delusions. However, the police surgeon, called to give evidence by Mr Ashton, said that the delusions were due only to drink.

After a retirement of ten minutes, the jury returned to court with a verdict of guilty. Mr Justice McCardie then passed the automatic sentence of death by hanging.

In the days before the execution, Herbert Salisbury made it known that he did not wish to appeal against his conviction or sentence, neither did he look for a reprieve from his fate. Salisbury was reported to have said: 'I shot her and I wish to die. I have nothing to live for now.'

It was customary to allow the passage of three Sundays between a death sentence and its execution. Herbert Salisbury was hanged at Walton at

8 a.m. on Thursday 11 May 1920. Only a few workmen stood outside the main gate of the prison in Hornby Road. Just before 8.30 a.m., the official notice of execution, signed by the prison governor, the chaplain and the under-sheriff of the county, was posted on the gate. For a moment, two passing workmen stopped to read it. Hanged with Salisbury, in a double execution on the same gallows, was William Waddington, an Oldham mill worker, for the murder of a seven-year-old girl.

Young Lovers

Unresolved powerful emotions can often result in violent acts, particularly in the young and in those who are emotionally vulnerable. Such consequences are featured in our second story, set in Oxton, Birkenhead, in the spring of 1920.

Elsie Birkett and Frank Andersen, both age 18, were sweethearts. Elsie lived with her parents at 25 Fairview Road, Oxton, This was one of a row of cottages, standing well up on the Oxton ridge, in front of which were long neatly kept gardens where tulips, lupins, marguerites and wallflowers grew. The little terrace overlooked the Tranmere valley, the hill beyond, and right onwards to the Mersey. Frank lived at 20 Sun Street in Birkenhead.

For some months, Frank had been calling on Elsie and walking out with her. It was clear that the young couple had become deeply attached to each other. Elsie, the youngest daughter of a gardener, was a daily domestic servant at 12 Normanton Road and she returned to Fairview Road each night. Frank had worked as a ship's steward. He was the son of a bargeman, the eighth of ten children. His broad features showed his Danish descent.

At about 12.15 p.m. on the afternoon of Sunday 25 April, while people were quietly returning home from morning church services, Elsie Birkett was seen running from Mount Pleasant into Poplar Road. When the girl had run about twenty yards, she staggered and fell, wounded, stabbed to the heart. Following behind Elsie was Frank Andersen. He was seen to kneel by the girl's side, apparently unfastening the collar of her now bloodstained white blouse. Just at this moment, a car drew up, driven by medical student James Oldham who was on his way home to Poplar Road. Oldham got out of the car and bundled the couple into it. He drove them both to the Borough Hospital. There it was found that the girl had died. The lad was wounded in the chest, but not seriously. On the spot where Elsie fell was found a very sharp sheath knife. Frank Andersen was detained in hospital under police custody.

Although the couple had been devoted sweethearts for some time, the courtship had been marred by several curious incidents. Young Andersen, although of sturdy physique, had been suffering from a very severe form of neurasthenia. His parents thought little of several remarks he had occasionally passed, but these remarks helped to cast some light on his poor state of health.

When Andersen was arrested at the Borough Hospital on 25 April, two letters, one of which was addressed to his parents, were found in his possession. They illustrated Andersen's despair and a degree of confusion. The first letter read:

> Dear Mother and Dad, Try and forgive me for what I am going to do, or if you can't forgive try and forget me. When you get this I will have signed on my long trip to another world. May God bless you and keep you in comfort in your old age. Give my love to all, your broken son, Frank.

Andersen's second letter, addressed 'To whom it may Concern', read as follows:

> Elsie is the cause of this, what I am about to do. I was all right till I met her, but I am a wreck, physical and mental. I told her of the state I was in six months ago, that I would have to go away for a time to get better. Elsie said she would rather die with me if I did not go away. She said she would die with me and could not live without me. I meant to finish it all some weeks ago, but Elsie kept on asking me to wait a little longer. Last night I meant it, but Elsie wanted to draw out at the last minute. She presented such a sorry spectacle of terror that I relented, and in the end I let her go, but as I write this I now I can't wait for my Elsie. I will kill her at the

first possible chance. Once I did not want her to come with me, but with her always imploring me to let her come. I have always looked upon it as the only thing. Elsie had took my life just as surely as if she had shot me. Therefore I am going to take hers not because of hatred or revenge, but because I can't do without her. God help me and give me strength to do it. My last wish is to be laid to rest with my Elsie and I know Elsie wishes it – Frank L. Andersen.

On Tuesday 27 April, an inquest was opened at Birkenhead by the Borough Coroner, Mr Cecil Holden. Elsie's mother, Mary Jane Birkett, had identified the body of her daughter. Mrs Birkett told the court that she last saw Elsie at 9 a.m. on the Sunday of the tragedy as she left for work. Coroner Holden said it appeared as if Andersen, who was still in hospital, stabbed the girl and then turned the weapon on himself, in an attempt to take his own life. 'In a statement to a police officer', said Mr Holden, 'he admitted stabbing the girl.' The inquest was adjourned for ten days.

On Friday 30 April, after being discharged from medical care at the hospital, Frank Andersen was formally charged with murder. He was then taken to the Birkenhead Police Court to appear before the magistrates. When he entered the dock, he walked to the bar rather stiffly. He had seemingly not yet fully recovered from his self-inflicted stab wound. Although rather flushed in appearance, he showed no outward sign of nervousness. Andersen was remanded in custody for a week pending further police inquiries.

Before Andersen could face a murder trial, there had to be a committal hearing, at which the evidence for the prosecution would be rehearsed, in order to see if a *prima facie* case existed against him. Although Andersen already stood charged with murder, an inquest jury had to arrive at a verdict as to the cause of death. It was at this inquest that the full facts of the case were first aired to public scrutiny, on 7 May 1920.

At the resumption of the inquest in the Birkenhead Police Court, Andersen was remanded for a further week. Pale and nervous, he smiled wanly at some friends in court. Coroner Holden directed him to sit with his solicitor in the well of the courtroom.

The first witness was Mrs Birkett. Questioned by the coroner, she said that her daughter had been keeping company with Andersen since the Christmas of 1919. He had not been working lately. She said he

Neurasthenia (Shell Shock)

Neurasthenia is now referred to as Post-Traumatic Stress Disorder. The condition has both physical and mental symptoms: fatigue, palpitations, hyperventilation, weakness, faintness, hysteria, delusions, paralysis and loss of speech.

During the course of the First World War the condition was recognised and taken seriously. The initial harsh judgements made towards men that they were malingerers or cowards was rejected as the numbers of sufferers grew. Nurses gave descriptions of shell-shocked behaviour, resembling epileptic fits, violent shivering and shaking. Some would have hallucinations and others could be a danger to themselves or others, having completely lost their minds.

The original form of treatment for sufferers of war neurosis was very harsh, including electric shock treatment, solitary confinement and stern emotional treatment. Eventually psychologists recognised that a different approach was required to alleviate and cure the condition.

It is estimated that 7–10% of officers and 3–4% of other ranks were affected by shell-shock. Four years after the end of the war there were 50,000 men in receipt of war pensions on mental health grounds.

seemed all right until about a month earlier, when she noticed him becoming 'sullen, morose and nervous in his manner'. On Saturday evening, 24 April, Elsie came home form her work with Andersen, and later they went out together. Elsie did not return home that night until after midnight, when Mrs Birkett noticed she had a scratch on her hand which was bleeding.

Eyewitnesses to the events of Sunday morning gave evidence. John Roberts, of Gorsefield Road, said that he was in Popular Road on the Sunday when he saw Frank and Elise standing at the corner of Mount Pleasant. They were facing each other, the girl's shoulder leaning against a wall. As he watched the couple, Roberts noticed that Andersen was smiling 'in a sinister way' and, as Roberts passed them, he looked at the girl and saw that she looked very hurt, as though whatever was being said to her was painful to hear.

Miss Hannah Dean of Rich View, Mount Pleasant, said that on the Sunday she saw Elsie in Mount Pleasant, running towards Poplar Road, and being followed by Andersen. The girl turned round, spoke some 'confidential words' to him and then ran on down Poplar Road. Again Andersen followed. Miss Dean noticed that Elsie looked very pale and 'her pallor was increasing'. After going a few yards down Poplar Road, the girl fell. Andersen knelt down beside her, raised her head, and unfastened her collar.

James Oldham, of Yew Tree, Poplar Road, testified that when he got out of his car he found the girl lying on her back. Andersen was lying on the pavement as well. Oldham could see blood on the girl's blouse and on the man's right hand. When he pulled the man away, a sheath knife was revealed, lying on the ground.

Oldham went for Dr Cassels Brown, who lived a few doors away in Poplar Road. Dr Brown came and attended to the girl. Dr Brown, in evidence, said, 'She was obviously dying. After a little while she gave on gasp and died'. He examined the man and found a puncture wound in his chest. Oldham then took the girl's body, along with Andersen, in his car to the Borough Hospital.

After the coroner had read out Andersen's two letters, medical evidence was heard. Dr Preece, the police surgeon, said that a knife had passed through the fourth rib of the girl. Death was due to haemorrhage. Dr Cyril Gater, house surgeon at the Borough Hospital, said he examined Andersen and found a wound in his chest, about three-quarters of an inch wide, but not very deep. Dr Gater said that Andersen asked him, 'Is she alive?' Later on, according to the doctor, he said either 'Shall I swing for this?', or perhaps 'I suppose I shall swing for this'. Andersen asked the doctor for a cigarette and 'began to talk in a very disjointed way'.

Police Sergeant Stephenson said he saw Frank Andersen on the Sunday in the hospital. As soon as Stephenson went into the ward, Andersen asked him 'How is she?' The sergeant cautioned him and told him he had better not say anything because there might be a serious charge made against him. 'But I want to tell you all about it,' said the lad. Stephenson said he took down a statement which Andersen dictated to him. The statement, which gave Andersen's version of what happened, ran as follows:

> I met my young lady Elsie Birkett at 25 Fairview Road. She resides there with her parents. I met her about 11 this morning at 12 Normanton Road, and she promised to meet me at 12 noon. I met her shortly after 12 at the top of Victoria Mount, and asked her to come for a walk for a few minutes with me and then go back home. She came. We walked round and got into Popular Road. We stood talking and making arrangements to meet tonight, But she refused to see me, saying her mother would not let her.

The statement ended thus: 'I then stabbed her. I meant it for her heart. I went all funny and don't know what I did after. I tried to stab myself, but it must have caught a bone. I was sorry, and tried to take her to a doctor.' The inquest was adjourned.

On the resumption of the inquest on 11 May, the coroner, in his summing up, said: 'the question of sanity or insanity has nothing to do with this court. It will be decided at the court before which the accused will be tried.' As was expected, after a short retirement, the inquest jury brought in a verdict of 'murder against Frank Lawrence Andersen'. Three days later, Andersen was committed for trial to Chester Assizes, reserving his defence.

The trial was held at Chester Castle Court on Friday 9 July 1920. Counsel for the prosecution was Mr T. Artemus Jones. Defending Andersen was Mr Austin Jones. After the prosecution had concluded its case, it was clear that Andersen had struck the fatal knife blow. In an attempt to save the young man's life, Austin Jones presented an insanity defence. After this it would be for the jury alone to decide, on the evidence, whether he had succeeded in proving that his client was insane.

In Anderson's favour was Mrs Birkett's statement that she had always found him 'a very decent and respectable young man'. She had, she said, offered no objection to his keeping company with her daughter. On the day of the tragedy she did not think there was 'anything peculiar about him', but he was, she said, 'very quiet'.

Andersen's father, Gustave, told the court that when Frank was about fifteen he joined the SS *Justinian* as an assistant steward. He was in that ship when she was torpedoed and after that, said Mr Andersen, his son was 'greatly shattered'. Later on, Frank got jobs on other ships until, in March 1919, he went on the *Grampian*, in which he made several voyages. In July of that year the ship ran into an iceberg off Newfoundland. Several men were killed and Frank was on duty at the time. After he came home to Birkenhead his health had 'completely changed'. One of his other sons, said Mr Andersen, was at present an inmate in a lunatic asylum. One of his daughters had attended a school for mental defectives.

Dr W. N. East, called for the defences, was a medical officer at Walton Prison. He said that during the time Andersen had been under his charge he had improved in health. Dr East considered that Andersen's 'emotionalisms and anxiety to die' were chiefly due to the effects of the experiences he had undergone at sea. The doctor said that personally he thought that Andersen was going to become insane. 'If I had seen him before the tragedy I would have certified him insane', said Dr East.

In his final remarks to the jury on behalf of Andersen, Mr Austin Jones submitted that at the time Andersen struck the fatal blow he was suffering from a mental disorder 'so great that he was insane and unable to appreciate what he was doing'.

Andersen was found 'guilty but insane' and ordered to be detained 'during his Majesty's pleasure' at a secure hospital. As he left the dock, Frank Andersen waved a hand to someone in the public gallery and smiled.

A Broken Vow

This case illustrates the fact that drunkenness was not a valid defence to a charge of murder. Although alcohol can lead to violence, it had no mitigating effect in law upon any reckless actions which might lead to an individual taking a life. Should defence counsel submit that his client's blame is lessened by having consumed alcohol, the judge in the case is duty bound to tell the jury to disregard it, or at the most to give the submission little or no weight in the determination of their verdict.

This story spotlights a disagreement between two lovers who had broken off their relationship, but between whom there was what might be called 'unfinished business', together with a good deal of bad feeling.

In the summer of 1920, a middle-aged widow called Mary Meakins lived at 6 House, 12 Court, off Hopwood Street in the Scotland Road district of Liverpool. Mrs Meakins had for the previous six years been living with another widow called Catherine Augood. Mary's husband had worked as a carter for a brewery, delivering ale to public houses. She had a child who was living with Mary's mother, Mrs O'Shea, in the Poplar district of London.

Mary Meakins had been friendly with a 43-year-old man called John Fitzgerald, a single man who was living at a lodging house called Bevington House in Limekiln Lane. After a dispute between the couple on Saturday 31 July, following drinking sessions in Great Crosshall Street and elsewhere, John took Mary's life in a house at 19 Byrom Terrace. On the following Monday, John Fitzgerald came before the Liverpool Stipendiary Magistrate on a charge of wilful murder. He was remanded in custody at Walton until 6 August.

On that day, Fitzgerald was present at the police court for the resumption of an inquest into Mary Meakins' death. Deputy City Coroner F. J. Leslie presided. He questioned the witnesses involved in the tragedy.

Mrs Augood, Mary Meakins' live-in companion, said that earlier in the year, Mary had confided to her that she expected to one day marry John Fitzgerald. She introduced him to her as 'my young man'. They always seemed to be on good terms, according to Mrs Augood. However, Mary had told her John had threatened that, if he found her in the company of any other man, he would either shoot her or cut her throat.

Before Mary became involved with John Fitzgerald she had been having a relationship with a man called James Dunford, a dock labourer. In December 1919 Mary had quarrelled with Dunford and finished their affair but, sometime in the summer of 1920, they ironed out their differences and began to see each other again, leaving Fitzgerald 'out in the cold'. It was jealousy of Dunford, compounded by a rejection by Mary, that supplied the driving force for the murder.

On Saturday night, about 9 p.m., Catherine Augood met Mary and

Dunford outside a café in Whitechapel, where they had drinks together. While they were sitting in a pub in Great Crosshall Street, Fitzgerald came in and asked Mary if he could buy her a drink. According to Mrs Augood, Mary replied, 'No thank you. Go away. I am finished with you'. Mary added something about a letter Fitzgerald had sent to her, and then she refused to shake hands with him.

Later on in the evening, after the pub had closed, a party of friends went to the house of a Mr and Mrs Nealen at 19 Byrom Terrace. Here, more drink was consumed and a sing-song developed. At about 11 p.m. Fitzgerald came in, had some drink and sang a song. According to Mrs Augood, as Fitzgerald was singing he walked towards Mary Meakins as though to shake hands. Mary moved back from him and said, 'I don't want anything to do with you'. Sensing that the party had come to an end, Mrs Nealen said, 'It's time you were going'.

Mary Meakins then picked up Mrs Nealen's baby and was kissing it when Fitzgerald walked across the room and put an arm round her. According to Mrs Augood, Fitzgerald then pressed Mary's head back with one hand and pulled his other hand out of a pocket. He made a quick movement and said 'I'll cut your throat'. Although Mrs Augood saw nothing in Fitzgerald's hand, Mary staggered across the room, bleeding from a throat wound. She collapsed shortly afterwards, and was dead by the time she reached the David Lewis Northern Hospital.

James Dunford, who had replaced John Fitzgerald in Mary's affections, gave his evidence at the inquest. Dunford said that he first met Mary at a World's Fair held in Scotland Road while he was on leave from his army unit in France. After that, said Dunford, 'We met frequently, but after a while we had a difference and ceased making appointments'. One day in July, Dunford came across Mary again. She was with Fitzgerald. Mary left the two men for a few minutes and Fitzgerald, whom he had never seen before, said ruefully, 'Women and wine, Jimmy'. To this remark Dunford replied, 'They're bad things'.

Dunford said that since that day he had met Mary Meakins every night. and stated, 'We intended to get married as soon as we could find apartments'. On the Saturday in question, Dunford and Mary met by appointment. Dunford's evidence as to what happened in the room at 19 Byrom Terrace tallied with Mrs Augood's version of events. According to Dunford, after the injury was inflicted on Mary's throat, Fitzgerald said, 'I have done her in'. Dunford could see an open razor in Fitzgerald's hand.

According to Mrs Nealen, the hostess of the rather drunken get-together at Byrom Terrace, a member of the party sang a song entitled 'Speak not her name'. The chorus included the passage 'I loved her well; she broke her vow'. When the song had finished, Fitzgerald repeated this line to Mary Meakins. He then jumped to his feet and addressing Mary he declared, 'That's what you have done to me'. A little later Mary said she was leaving, and waltzed blithely around the table to kiss Mrs Nealen's baby. She next had the child in her arms, holding it up above her head.

It was at that moment, said Mrs Nealen, that Fitzgerald caught hold of Mary's neck, and inflicted a deep razor wound across her throat. The only words which Mary uttered after she had been cut were to the little baby: 'Kiss me, Chuck'.

Deputy Coroner Leslie read out in court a letter, written by Fitzgerald

to Mary on 21 July, just ten days before her death. In the letter, reference was made to a previous message from the spurned and contrite lover. The letter read as follows:

> Dear Mary, I received your letter this morning, and I cannot express my sorrow at the pain it must have put you to by sending to you that letter. I was under the influence of drink when I wrote it, and I am extremely sorry for what I wrote to you. Dear Mary, I do hope and trust that you will forgive me for what I said. Good God! I must be mad to say such a thing about you, so I hope to God you will forgive me. If it is a thing that we have to part, then let us part as friends and not as enemies. I have not rested thinking about the letter. I will conclude by wishing you good night and God bless you, Mary. XXX

During the reading of his letter, Fitzgerald burst into tears and buried his face in his hands.

Two young men had accompanied Fitzgerald on his way to give himself up at the main bridewell. One said that Fitzgerald told him, 'I have been living with her for twelve months and she has been living with other men while I was away'. To the other man, he was alleged to have said, 'I had just taken her for a week's holiday, and when we came back she told me she was going for a month's holiday with another fellow'.

At the bridewell, Fitzgerald was dealt with by Detective Sergeant Kelly. He said that at midnight on the Saturday, he saw that Fitzgerald had been drinking and 'appeared dazed'. 'I have cut her throat. Is she dead?', he asked. Kelly replied 'Yes'. Fitzgerald was then said to have declared: 'I suppose I'll hang'. At 7 a.m. the following morning, when Fitzgerald was sober, Kelly charged him with murder, whereupon Fitzgerald apparently said, 'Wilful murder? I remember nothing about it. I was drunk'.

John Fitzgerald was tried at St George's Hall before Mr Justice Greer on Friday 29 October 1920. He pleaded 'not guilty'. Outlining the case against Fitzgerald, prosecuting counsel Merriman said it was 'an illustration of the eternal triangle'. For the defence, Mr Madden decided not to put Fitzgerald into the witness box. Instead, he called evidence to show that his client had been drinking heavily immediately before the tragedy. 'Ordinarily', said Mr Madden, 'he was a mild and inoffensive man'.

Dr East, medical officer at Walton Prison, who had kept the accused man under observation since his committal for trial, said that Fitzgerald was 'suffering from a very advanced valvular disease of the heart which might prove fatal at any moment'. Dr East then said that 'In the closing stages of the disease there might be delirium, hallucinations, and morbid impulses, though it is only rarely that the disease produces these effects'. Crucially, Dr East confessed that he had not found evidence of any form of mental defect in Fitzgerald.

Mr Madden, in his final speech for the defence, declared: 'I do not attempt to controvert the proposition of the prosecution that it was Fitzgerald's hand that took the life of the woman. The prisoner, however, was very drunk at the time. There can be no doubt that all the parties concerned had had quite as much drink as was good for them'.

Hinting at an insanity plea Mr Madden said,

> There is a great difference between cold-blooded, intentional murder, and the unfortunate taking of a fellow creature's life, by one who was either drunk or in delirium, or one whose mind was in some way unbalanced.

The jury were twenty minutes in considering their verdict, after which their foreman announced that they found him 'Guilty'. Fitzgerald received the death sentence calmly and, as he left the dock for his cell below, he waved to friends at the back of court.

All, however, was not lost for John Fitzgerald. A petition bearing some 25,000 signatures, appealing against capital punishment and pleading for clemency for the condemned man, was sent to the Home Secretary. The execution had been arranged for 16 November but just three days earlier, on Saturday 13 November, Fitzgerald's sentence was commuted to one of penal servitude for life. At nearly the last moment, Fitzgerald had received a merciful release from his fate.

The Possessive Lodger

On the night of Saturday 9 April 1921, at about 11.30 p.m., Albert Appleton, a man in his seventies, was walking home towards his house in Newby Street, off Walton Lane, near the Everton football stadium. As he approached number 89, Mr Appleton heard raised quarrelling voices. In the dim street light he could see that a man and a woman were arguing with each other by the front door of the house. A man's voice said: 'I will go', and Mr Appleton saw him step back a couple of feet from the woman, who had he backed to the doorway. Suddenly a gunshot rang out in the still night air. The woman fell, crying, 'What have you done this for?' While she lay on the ground, the gunman fired four more shots in quick succession, and ran off towards Walton Lane.

Several neighbours emerged from their front doors to see what had happened. Lying in front of her door at 89 Newby Street was someone they knew well: Mrs Olive Duff. Taken aback by the swiftness of events, Albert Appleton shouted' 'Stop that man, he has fired five shots into a woman!' Chase was given by several neighbours, but the man, whose face no one managed to see, made good his escape.

After hearing the gunshots, a police constable with the number 257E on his epaulets, on his way home from duty, saw a man moments later running down Langham Street and into an entry. The police officer took up the chase along the alleyway, but when he emerged into the street again the fugitive had disappeared into the night. Not knowing the way the man had taken, the officer made his way in the direction of the shots to give help at the crime scene back in Newby Street.

Olive Duff, bleeding from a chest wound, was carried into her house. After losing consciousness she was taken by ambulance to Stanley Hospital. As was feared, when she arrived there she was already dead. Every one of the gunshots had made its mark on Mrs Duff. She had a bullet wound in each hand, one in the back of the right shoulder, and one just above the left elbow.

Olive Duff's real name was Jackson. For the previous twelve years Olive, a widow, had been living with George William Duff as his wife.

Her two sons and two daughters, who had been brought up by Duff, had been under the impression that he was their stepfather. At the time of the shooting, Duff was 60 and Olive Jackson was 44.

Also living in the terraced house in Newby Street was a 43-year-old lodger, a ship's steward by the name of Thomas Wilson. He had been in the household for more than five years. During that time Wilson had established a somewhat unconventional relationship with Olive and George. Wilson and the Duffs often used to go out as a threesome, and at other times Wilson and Olive went out together as a couple, to pubs and to the cinema. Often, during Wilson's free time between voyages, he and Olive would go out together on shopping expeditions. Occasionally, Wilson would buy presents for Olive or for the children. George Duff believed that Olive was safe in Wilson's company and was pleased that they got on so well together. Exactly how close was the relationship between Olive and Wilson remains unclear, but by all accounts Wilson was devoted to his landlady. As it turned out, his devotion had resulted in her violent death; it was Wilson who shot Olive and ran away on the Saturday night.

That night, Thomas Wilson slept fitfully in a room at the Commercial Hotel in Lime Street, having signed the register 'Thomas Smith'. The police, based on what Wilson had said, believed that he would try to make his way to London, so two detectives were put on special duty to keep watch for Wilson at Lime Street Station. At about 11.45 a.m. on the Sunday, Wilson entered the station from Lord Nelson Street. When he saw the detectives, he turned on his heels and beat a hasty retreat. The police, thinking that Wilson might have recognised them, ran after him, Detective Cox in the lead. When they caught up with him, Wilson put both of his hands in his overcoat pockets. Fearing an attack, Sergeant Owen drew a revolver and called out, 'Hands up!' Wilson readily complied and was then arrested.

As Wilson and the two detectives were crossing Lime Street, and before anything had been said as to the cause of his arrest, Wilson was alleged to have asked: 'How is she?' 'Who?' replied Owen. 'Mrs Duff'. When told she was dead, Wilson is said to have exclaimed: 'My God! This is through drink and the others!'

Nearing the Cheapside bridewell, the sergeant, rather belatedly it would seem, asked Wilson if he had a revolver. Wilson told him that he did. It was in his right-hand trouser pocket, an automatic pistol with one bullet left in it. On the seaman's identity certificate which was found on him, Wilson had written a statement headed, 'My will'. It went on: 'I wish to leave my money to Norman Jackson and my rings to Mr Duff. My money is in Spellow Lane bank. This trouble is all over Harry, as I told Mr Duff, that his wife refused to come home. She has been in my company for six years. She has never left me before'.

On the Monday morning, 11 April, Wilson was brought before the stipendiary magistrate at the police court, charged with the wilful murder of Olive Duff. Wilson, clean-shaven and sandy-haired, looked much younger than his given age of 43. Giving evidence of events, when Wilson was taken to the bridewell, Detective Chief Inspector Hughes said that he told Wilson that it would be necessary for him to give an account of his movements on the Saturday night. This was in spite of the fact that Wilson was, as yet, not represented by a solicitor.

According to DCI Hughes, Wilson made a long statement, detailing his dealings with Mrs Duff on the night of the shooting, up to the point when they reached the front gate of her house. The verbal evidence was that Wilson said to Hughes: 'She told me to beat it. I asked her if she meant that, and she replied: "If you like". Then I lost my temper and shot her, but I did not know she was dead.' In reply to a charge of wilful murder, Wilson replied, 'Very good, sir'.

Wilson was still unrepresented at the police court. Asked in court whether he had anything to say in regard to the application for a remand, Wilson said: 'I would like it over today if I could get it'. The magistrate replied, 'I am afraid I cannot do that for you'. A two-day remand was then ordered.

An inquest was opened on Wednesday 13 April. Before it started, Wilson was brought into court and remanded until 18 April. At the outset, DCI Hughes announced that the name of the dead woman had now been ascertained to be Jackson and not Duff. It had, said Hughes, been necessary to recharge Wilson. To this Wilson said: 'I knew that was her name'. Holding a watching brief on proceedings for George Duff was solicitor J. A. Behn. Wilson was alone, still unrepresented.

George Duff was the first witness at the inquest. He was a heavy thickset man who worked as a Customs Prevention Officer. He appeared to be greatly distressed.

As soon as Duff had sworn the oath in the witness box, he turned to face

Wilson, who was sitting between two policemen, a few yards away. Duff then shouted at Wilson in an angry voice: 'You murderer! You murderer!' At this, three court officials rushed to Duff's side and tried to restrain him. Wildly waving his arms, Duff had to be forcibly prevented from dashing out the box at the hapless Wilson. Duff now appeared to be on the verge of collapse. He crouched down in the witness box with a police officer supporting him. When raised to a sitting position Duff turned once more to Wilson and repeated his exclamations, shaking his fist threateningly at the accused man.

After a ten-minute adjournment to allow tempers to cool, Duff was heard to say that there was never 'anything wrong' between Olive and Wilson. Duff described his lodger as 'a hasty and excitable man'. He said he was 'fairly temperate, but he does occasionally get the worse for drink'.

Duff described how, on Saturday night, he met Olive and Wilson in the bar parlour of a public house in Walton Road. Whilst in the pub they were joined by a number of friends. They were together until closing time, all being 'in a friendly humour' according to Duff. Wilson drank rum, a drink which he did not usually have; he mentioned that he was drinking it 'for a cold'.

When the party left the pub at 10 p.m., they were all invited to go round to the nearby house of Mr and Mrs Hooley. Feeling tired, Duff Went home. Wilson, 'under the influence of drink but not drunk' according to Duff's testimony, went with him. Duff went straight to his bed. The next thing he remembered was being called down to help Olive, who was lying in the garden near the front gate.

Wilson was asked if he wished to put any questions to Duff. He replied in the negative. Another rumpus then broke out in the court. Duff still bore traces of his earlier agitation and as he left the witness box and passed behind Wilson, he tried to break loose from the officer who was leading him out of court. He tried to strike Wilson but before he could achieve this, another two officers seized him and forcibly removed him. Duff continued to put up a violent struggle. Outside the court, he collapsed in a heap on a bench.

Norman Jackson, Olive's 21-year-old son, was the next witness. He said he met his mother and Wilson in the pub and stayed with them for about a quarter of an hour before going home to Newby Street. At about 11.30 he heard gunshots at the front of the house and, rushing out of the door, promptly tripped over the body of his mother, who was lying at the bottom of the garden passage near the gate. The young man said that Wilson was a man of very hasty temper. But, said Jackson, 'he was a friendly man and always seemed ready to go anywhere with me'.

Wilson was allowed to question each witness at the end of their stint in the witness box. This gave rise to a series of inane questions. To Norman Jackson Wilson said: 'If you thought that Duff was your stepfather, why did you not take his name, and not the name of Jackson?' Norman replied: 'Well, naturally I would take my mother's name, wouldn't I?'

A young daughter, also called Olive, was very distraught as she gave her evidence, and it was only with great difficulty that she managed to speak at all. She said that Wilson had always been treated like one of the family, but that he lost his temper very easily if anything happened that was not to his liking. Evidently, Wilson was something of a prude. Olive recalled a Christmas party at the house when Wilson was very much annoyed when a man called Harry Roskell kissed all the girls under the mistletoe.

Wilson interrupted young Olive by saying to her: 'I wasn't at home at Christmas time. It must have been the New Year's party.' 'Well, it was the night I mean', the girl replied. Ever the gallant, Wilson did not ask the girl anything else. 'The girl is too ill', he explained.

Emily Besant, a friend of the dead woman, had been staying with the Duffs for several weeks. She confirmed that Wilson returned home with Mr Duff, soon after 10 p.m. on the Saturday evening. Duff went straight to bed, but Wilson, after going upstairs, went out again by the back way. She said, 'He seemed to be quite sober and in a normal mood.'

It seems that Harry Roskell, who had kissed the girls under the mistletoe, was really disliked by Thomas Wilson. It was possibly the enmity between the two men, mainly generated by Wilson, that led ultimately to the shooting. Mrs Caroline Lawson, a friend of Olive Jackson, and one of the drinking party, said that when it was suggested that they all should go to the house of the Hooleys, Wilson declined to go because, he said, he did not like Roskell, and would be sure to have a row with him if he went. Olive Duff then asked Wilson what he had against Roskell, and Wilson replied, 'He is too fond of kissing'.

According to Mrs Lawson, Wilson caught up with Olive Duff and Mrs Hooley. They had been standing for some time at the corner of Spellow

Lane. Mrs Lawson, who was waiting for a tramcar, overheard a conversation between the couple.

'I am not going to be dictated to by you', Duff said to Wilson.

'All right, I'll get the first train to London in the morning', he replied.

'You can get it tonight!', came the retort.

Mrs Hooley gave a further account of events. She said: 'We were all quite friendly until a visit to my house was suggested'. Wilson, she said, then appeared to be 'nasty in his temper'. As Mrs Hooley was walking with Mrs Duff through a passage leading to Spellow Lane, Wilson sprang out on them unexpectedly. He asked Olive, in a threatening manner, where she was going.

'Mr Duff sent me to look after you.'

'I don't believe he would do such a thing', Olive replied.

More harsh words passed between them and then Olive snarled: 'Why, if my husband died tonight I would not marry a worm like you!'

The mysterious kisser, Harry Roskell, a fruit seller who lived at 2 Elphin Grove, off Luxmore Road in Walton, said that he knew Thomas Wilson 'only very slightly'. He had, he insisted, never given him any cause for dislike. Until now, he said, he did not know that Wilson had any reason to be jealous of him. It was soon to become clear that Wilson did bear a grudge against Roskell.

'On the night of the party you got hold of Ma and kissed her?'

'I have no recollection of that at all', replied Roskell.

'You tried several times to kiss her, and she told you to cut it out.'

'I never did', replied Roskell, 'and I have never given you cause for jealousy in any shape or form.'

In his testimony, Detective Chief Inspector Hughes said Wilson told him that when they all left the pub, Olive insisted on going to the party at the Hooleys. Wilson then came home and got the gun. He went after Olive and met her in Spellow Lane. Wilson said he persuaded her not to go to the party and they went home together. As they reached the house, they were quarrelling, and this led to the shooting. Wilson said that with his money in the bank he wanted a grave to be bought for Olive.

Medical evidence was called. It was stated that a bullet had pierced Olive's heart. Asked if he had any questions to put to the doctor, Wilson replied, 'No, I stand on my own'. The coroner asked him: 'Do you want to make any statement for yourself?'

'No, sir', replied Wilson. The inquest jury returned a verdict of wilful murder against Wilson. He was then committed for trial on a coroner's warrant.

Because the Liverpool Spring Assizes had only recently ended, Wilson faced his trial at Manchester. It was 2 May 1921. The case against Wilson was made crystal clear by prosecuting Counsel A. J. Ashton KC. For the defence, Mr Madden called no evidence. In his appeal to the jury, Mr Madden said: 'On the night of the shooting there was no murder in the heart of the accused. It would be idle for me to say that the prisoner's hand was not the one that fired the pistol, but has Wilson committed murder?'

Hoping perhaps to obtain at least a recommendation for mercy from the jury, Mr Madden finished his appeal by saying:

> For years I have been an apostle crying in the wilderness for the alteration of the law with regard to murder. There must be intent to commit murder, full and complete, before you can find a person guilty, and as long as you are satisfied that there is not that intent, then even at this time, I am entitled to demand a verdict of manslaughter at your hands.

Wilson was found guilty of murder and sentenced to death. He was hanged at Strangeways Gaol, Manchester, on the morning of 25 May 1921.

John Brown's Body

Mary Pannell lived with her husband and her married daughter in the basement of 14 Brownlow Street, off Pembroke Place, by the old Royal Infirmary. In her sixties, Mrs Pannell used to sublet the upstairs rooms of no. 14 and, in May 1921, she put an advertisement into the *Liverpool Echo* for a vacancy she had for a ground floor back room at ten shillings a week.

A few days later, Mrs Pannell let the room to a man who gave his name as John Brown.

Mr Brown told Mrs Pannell that all he required was sleeping accommodation. He said he would be out during the daytime as he was a commercial traveller in women's wear. The next day he moved in with several parcels. Mrs Pannell gave him a latch key and a key to his room. Brown spoke with a foreign accent and had a habit of shrugging his shoulders and gesticulating when he did speak and Mrs Pannell got the impression that Brown was probably French. Perhaps because he was a foreigner, thought Mary Pannell, he did not seem very fond of English conversation. Brown did like to keep himself very much to himself, and he became quite irritable on the few occasions when Mrs Pannell and her daughter Florrie disturbed him in his room.

Mrs Pannell began to look upon John Brown as an ideal tenant. He was out of the house every day, from breakfast time until about 11 p.m., and more than once he stayed away altogether for two or three days at a time. Moreover, Brown was always punctual in paying his rent, a fact which pleased Mrs Pannell no end. Every Wednesday morning he went to the top of the stairs leading to the basement, which Mrs Pannell reserved for her own use, and called down to her: 'Missus, your money!'

Mrs Pannell soon noticed that when Brown went out he always bolted his door, but he never locked it. About a fortnight after he moved in, Brown stayed away for five or six nights. He said he had been to visit his sister, who was an army officer's widow and very ill, with only the neighbours to attend to her.

John Brown's sister later visited him at Brownlow Street on about three occasions. Mrs Pannell contrived to meet her and was very impressed. Her name was May. She was about 40, Mrs Pannell thought, and very attractive, with dark hair, a fresh complexion and a slender face with high cheekbones. She was always fashionably dressed but, Mary noticed disapprovingly, she used quite a lot of make-up. She also had a full set of false teeth. Not being familiar with May's unusual accent, Mrs Pannell put this down to being, like her brother, a foreigner.

At about 3.30 p.m. on Friday 15 July, May, who had a very pleasing manner, called at 14 Brownlow Street. The landlady's daughter, Florrie Wright, answered the door. May asked Florrie if she might see 'my brother Jack'. At the same moment, Brown opened the door of his room and asked the woman in. Florrie admired her lovely clothes. She was wearing a light silver-grey costume, with a fancy red silk handkerchief in the breast pocket. She wore a grey velour hat with a silk hatband patterned with flowers. The ensemble was completed by high-legged leather boots with shiny patent toecaps. She looked 'a picture', according to Florrie.

At about 4 p.m. Brown's sister went to the top of the basement stairs and asked for two plates and two spoons, saying that she and her brother were going to eat some fruit, before going into the city to dine. It was a sunny summer's afternoon and so Florrie decided to sit out in the back yard. May joined Florrie in the yard and asked her if she could stay there a while because, she said, her brother was shaving. 'I have a horror of razors', she said.

Eventually, Brown and his sister went out. Before Brown had come back home, the Pannells and their daughter went to bed, believing that Brown would follow his usual practice and would let himself in about 11 p.m. Soon after 9 a.m. on the Saturday morning, Brown left the house as usual. However, on this occasion, he locked the door of his room, something he never did. As far as anyone knew, John Brown never came back to the house again.

Brown's absence raised no suspicions. After all, he had often gone away for two or three days at a time. However, by the following Wednesday Brown had failed to pay his week's rent. Five days had now elapsed without any sight of him. Moreover, Mrs Pannell noticed an objectionable smell in the region of Brown's room. Although the door was locked and Brown had the key, Mrs Pannell decided the room had to be cleaned whether he liked her entering or not. Another lodger, an army pensioner called Bill Grant, by means of a ladder climbed through the room's window. It was some height above the level of the back yard.

When Mr Grant got into Brown's room, he found it in a state of disorder. However, Grant's attention was drawn at once to the bed. At the pillow end, the clothes and mattress were soaked in blood. The police were called.

A person's leg was sticking out from beneath the bedstead. Under the bed, up against the wall, was the body of a woman, almost decapitated by two fearsome gashes across her throat. There was a shocking mutilation of the body, a part being removed and placed elsewhere.

Two of the dead woman's fellow lodgers who lived with her at 22 Springfield Street, near St Anne's Street, recognised the clothing at 14 Brownlow Street as belonging to a woman they knew as Mary McKenzie. Later, at the mortuary, the two women confirmed their belief by inspecting other items of apparel. Facial changes had set in to such an extent that identification by the body alone could not be satisfactorily established. There was no doubt that the dead woman was Mary McKenzie. She had discussed Brown with her friends and had said that she was going to his room on the Friday night to collect some underclothing which he had bought for her.

When the police forced an entry into the room of death at Brownlow Street, they found Mary McKenzie's body in a pool of blood, clad in only a chemise. Two men's shirts had been thrown over her left shoulder. There was a big gash on the left side of her throat. On the mantelpiece, Detective Sergeant Whiteley found a bloodstained razor with pieces chipped out of it. Four long hairs adhered to the blade. In hindsight, the dead woman's fear of razors proved to have been justified. Underneath the bed, Whiteley found two plates of false teeth and another single tooth stuck to the blood on the blanket.

A vast quantity of shirts and collars, which had been stolen recently from cars in the city, to the value of £100, were also found in Brown's room. There were skeins of wool, ladies underwear, combs, studs and boxes of pins. Some of Mary McKenzie's clothes, which had been cut from her body, were stolen goods, with ten pairs of boots which had been taken from a firm in Castle Street. An empty lady's purse was found in the room.

The murderer, be he Brown or anyone else, had enjoyed a full five days in which to make good his escape. Mrs Pannell told the police that Brown had filled in a 1921 census paper with the name 'Edward Brown, 48, from London, a commercial traveller in woollen and cotton goods'. She took him to be French.

A nation-wide manhunt was set in motion to find the mysterious foreigner. The police circulated a description of the wanted man. This read:

> Between 40 and 50, 5ft 10in to 5ft 11in tall, broad set, sallow complexion, dark brown hair, a ragged moustache (turning slightly grey), wearing a dark grey mixture suit alternately with a very light grey suit and black bowler hat. He has a grey check cap and walks with a very slight stoop and a slouching gait.

Before and after the crime, Brown seems to have been very careful that little should be known of his private affairs. He received no letters at Brownlow Street, parcels left behind for him had the senders' addresses removed and there was destruction of some pages in a book which might have afforded a clue to the man's identity. Police did manage to trace some of Brown's customers, however, and from them they learned that he was known as E. Brown as well as John Brown. He used to wear high quality linen shirts with starched fronts, together with expensive boots. Police inquiries were extended to the continent under the supervision of Detective Superintendent McCoy.

On Saturday 23 July an inquest was opened by the Deputy City Coroner, Mr Mills Roberts. He told the inquest jury: 'There is no doubt that a foul murder has been committed'. The jury, as was then common practice, were taken to the mortuary to view the body.

The first person to go into the witness box was a Mrs Kelly of 19 Russell Street, off Brownlow Hill. She said she had known Mary McKenzie for about two and half years. Mrs Kelly told the court:

> She was a widow but when she came to me she represented herself to be single on account of her trying to obtain work. She stayed with me the first time for six months when she was working, and also since when she was out of a situation.

Mrs Kelly said that Mrs McKenzie lived at Russell Street on the last occasion until the June or July of 1920. She then left to work as head waitress at either Colwyn Bay or Llandudno, at the George's Hotel. Later, in the October, she returned to Mrs Kelly's house at the end of the summer hotel season. Later, May came 'backwards and forwards periodically'. Her dead husband was an engineer on a ship called the *Black Prince*. 'She went out everyday', said Mrs Kelly, 'and sometimes stayed out all night'. When Mrs Kelly last saw May she seemed 'lively and in good health'.

Mrs Kelly made the coroner very angry. She said she had identified the body at the mortuary by the high cheekbones and the shape of Mrs McKenzie's mouth. She then declared: 'I would have been more certain if I had seen her hands and legs'. Fuming, coroner Mills Roberts snapped at Mrs Kelly: 'Then you had better go back to the mortuary!' After mentioning that the victim's maiden name was Clarke and that she came from the Isle of Man, Mrs Kelly went, as instructed, back to the Prince's Dock mortuary. On returning to court she said she was now 'quite satisfied' as to the identity of the dead woman. The inquest was then adjourned.

The police manhunt continued. Clues were few, but they included a specimen of handwriting and, more particularly, a partly obliterated laundry mark on one of Brown's shirt collars. The police traced the mark to the laundry business of a Mrs Bertha McGibbon of 90 Breck Road, who had a shop at 68 Low Hill. Mrs McGibbon told police that twelve months earlier she had a laundry in Erskine Street and a man called E. Braen was one of her customers. About four months later she moved over to Low Hill and dealt with the same man. His name, she said, had then become E. Brown.

Braen was known to the Liverpool police as a native of Belgium. As luck would have it, they had photographs on file, a front and a side view of the suspect. It was believed that Braen had returned to Belgium to avoid arrest. Detective Superintendent McCoy and Inspector Jones crossed the channel to Antwerp, arriving there before any news of the pursuit had reached the Belgian police, so that Braen would not be so much on the alert.

At 6 a.m. on 29 July, McCoy went with a Belgian police officer called van Loon to a house in Antwerp. The two men arrested Braen and took him to the police office. When McCoy charged Braen with murder, he was alleged to have said: 'I knew at once what you wanted, but I did not do the murder. It was done by a man called Fisher who belongs to Manchester. I will not say anything more.'

A press release issued by the Liverpool police described the arrested man as Edouard Braen, aged 48, a capmaker, who had served in the Belgian Lancers during the war. Braen was kept in the custody of the Belgian police while plans were being activated to extradite him and bring him back to Liverpool.

On 10 August the Belgian authorities refused to extradite Braen. They said that he would have to be tried in Belgium, even though the crime had been committed in England, making it arguable that the case should be heard under English law. The Belgian prosecutor pointed out that the seventeen prosecution witnesses would have to travel to Antwerp for the trial. Testimony by written affidavit would not be acceptable.

The adjourned inquest was reopened on 11 August, at Liverpool. The coroner said that Mary McKenzie's real name was believed to be Clarke because she had never been married. Mrs Kelly gave more evidence and said that she had never seen Mrs McKenzie with anyone by the name of Fisher or Fischer. A brother of the dead woman, Hugh Clarke of Ballaugh, Isle of Man, had identified the body as his sister. Her real name was, he said, Sarah Mary Clarke. He last saw her eight years previously and had not heard from her since. At that time she was working as a waitress in Douglas and was single. 'I have heard of her marriage', said Clarke, 'but I am not certain that she was really married.' His sister was 47, he said.

Mary Ellen Smith, Mary's landlady at a lodging house at 22 Springfield Street, said that she had stayed with her for twelve months. Mrs Smith described her as 'a steady, moral woman'. She had seen her the worse for drink on only two occasions. Mary went out daily to do plain sewing and she also worked as a waitress. On Friday 15 July, the day of her disappearance, she told Mrs Smith that she was going out to meet 'her boy'. The same evening, Mrs Smith saw her with a man in the stalls of the

Rotunda Theatre. The man wore a grey suit and a straw hat. From police photographs Mrs Smith could not identify the man. However, both Mary Pannell and her daughter Florrie were able to identify Braen. 'That's the man', declared Florrie confidently.

Mrs McGibbon, the laundry lady, also identified Braen. He had, she said, at first given his address as 40 Guelph Street, but about 10 weeks previously ago he had changed it to Brownlow Street. On 14 July, the day before he disappeared, Braen brought in two collars and a singlet. Mrs McGibbon said she never saw him again.

From the witness box at the inquest, Superintendent McCoy read out a statement made on 30 July at the Court of First Instance in Antwerp. It was Braen's version of events at Brownlow Street which led up to the killing. Braen said he met Fisher in a bar in Lime Street. Fisher, he said, asked him to dispose of some stolen property. Mary McKenzie was introduced to him as a 'public woman' who would take messages from Fisher to Braen between their periodic meetings in pubs.

According to Braen, on the night of the 'accident' the three of them went into his room. Fisher and Mary began to quarrel over money which she said Fisher owed her. There was such a noisy altercation that Braen locked the door. Braen said that when he turned round, Fisher was cutting the woman's throat. They put the body under the bed, got between the sheets, and slept until early next morning, when they parted. Fisher, said Braen, was about 32 with bright blue eyes and fair hair, dressed in a blue suit. This account was to form the basis of Braen's defence at his trial.

Almost a year elapsed before Braen's trial opened at Antwerp, on 11 July 1922. The President of the Court opened the proceedings by interrogating the accused man. The President declared that he did not believe Braen. He suggested that Braen's statements about the man Fisher were 'complete inventions'.

Braen said he was born at Courtrai. In 1894 he was imprisoned at Morxplas. At the outbreak of war in 1914, after a short stay in Holland, he went to England, living at Liverpool, where Fisher employed him to sell clothing.

Because of the need to translate the evidence into French and English, the trial was prolonged until 14 July. At Liverpool a private detective called Arthur Lloyd Jones had been sent to look for the mysterious Fisher. He found three men of that name in Liverpool – George, Charles and Harry

Fisher. Charles Fisher had seen Braen for the last time on 21 July 1921. Harry Fisher said he had travelled with Braen from London to Liverpool and the next day went into hospital for ten weeks. He had not seen Braen again. Strangely enough, Braen said in court that he was unable to recognise the photographs of the three men.

After a half-hour's consideration, the Belgian jury found Braen guilty of wilful murder, as well as ten charges of theft and one of receiving stolen goods. The sentence was penal servitude for life with the loss of his political rights and the payment of the expenses of the trial, amounting to 27,400 francs (about £550).

Because there was no capital punishment in Belgium, Edouard Braen escaped with his life. Had he been tried in England, he would more than likely have paid the supreme penalty.

Armed Robbery

Just before 7 p.m. on the evening of 11 June 1923, two men entered the Hopwood Street sub post office at 360 Scotland Road. Serving inside the shop were a Miss Healy and Annie Lovelady, the postmistress's daughter. They were about to close the office for the day.

One of the men shut the door behind him and stood with his back to it. A lull of quietness fell over the room. The other man, taller than his companion, approached Miss Healy and said to her: 'We have come for the money'. Miss Lovelady moved towards the telephone as if to pick it up and then screamed for help to the living quarters above the shop. There was a small sum of money spread on the counter. The tall man picked up the money and pointed a revolver at Miss Lovelady. Meanwhile, the shorter man went out through the door, followed by Miss Healy. Just then, the postmistress's son Thomas came rushing downstairs into the shop and shouted to the gunman: 'Drop that money!' Thomas managed to force the gunman from behind the counter, whereupon he was shot in the abdomen at point blank range and fell to the floor.

A hue and cry was raised as the two robbers made their escape on foot. One of the robbers, who fled northwards, was now bare headed, as Annie had snatched his cap from his head as he went through the door. A chase began. The gunman made good his escape while the other man ran down Newsham Street, followed several passers-by and a man called James Cunliffe of 29 Everton Brow.

The fleeing man turned and fired shots at his pursuers but Cunliffe caught him and grabbed hold of his coat. The man then shot at Cunliffe through his pocket. The bullet went over Cunliffe's shoulder. According to his account, 'I then jumped on to the man's back and brought him down. The pistol was knocked out of his hand. We held him down until Police Constable Lewis arrived and handcuffed him'.

The man tried again to escape, but he received such a violent handling from the crowd, which included several burly dock labourers, that he seemed pleased finally to be led away by PC Lewis, assisted by several other officers. The captive was then taken to Rose Hill bridewell, followed by a crowd of about two hundred people. The revolver was found by a little boy and given to the police.

Thomas Lovelady, who had been shot during the raid, was rushed to the Stanley Hospital. Aged 22, he was a provender dealer with a store in William Moult Street. An accident when he was eight years old had rendered him blind in one eye and he had weak sight in the other.

On being searched, the captured man was found to be carrying a murderous implement in the shape of a ¾″ lead pipe packed with cotton and wire. In court on 12 June he gave his name as Albert Finchley of New Orleans and was remanded in custody for a week. The charge was the attempted murder of James Cunliffe.

Thomas Lovelady died from his wounds at 7.30 p.m. on 13 June, and the next day Finchley was charged with his wilful murder. This was in spite of the fact that he did not fire the fatal shot. As an accessory to the crime he was considered to be culpable of it, bearing in mind that the attempted raid on the post office was a joint venture by the two men, one of whom was still at large.

On the morning of Friday 15 June, two other men were in the dock at the Liverpool Police Court. They were John Brannigan, aged 30, a communist leader of Fell Street, and Augustine Power, aged 20, of Ople Street. They were charged with being in possession of explosives with intent to endanger life.

After his arrest, Albert Finchley, now known to be James Phelan, was said to have told the police that Brannigan and Power had explosives and firearms, one of the latter having killed Thomas Lovelady. The allegation

Firearms

Before 1920 there were no laws to regulate the purchase, possession or carrying (peacefully) of firearms in Britain. This legal right to own firearms was ended by the Firearms Act of 1920, and governments have continued to restrict legal access to guns and rifles to the present day.

There are a number of reasons given why this Act was passed. Troubles in Ireland were being fuelled by gun-running from the mainland. There were social and political upheavals before the First World War: rise of the Labour movement and party, the suffragette/suffragist campaigns and industrial action such as the Transport Strike of 1911, that unsettled the government. After the end of hostilities these activities resumed, one notable one being the Police Strike of 1918, heavily supported in Liverpool but also supported in Birmingham and London. Veterans of the war returning to unemployment and poverty, aware of the events in Russia in 1917 and the political upheavals in Europe at the end of the war were a concern for the government. Freely available guns and rifles could make the fears of social instability and revolution in Britain a reality. The Bolshevik revolution and its potential influence on the British population was of particular concern.

Though the reason for the Act was to remove weapons from the hands of burglars and other criminals, the fact that rifles were included in the legislation, weapons that were not easy to conceal but were used at a distance, suggest that there was a fear of political and social unrest that the presence of guns could exacerbate.

against Brannigan was that Phelan asked him if he had any guns as he wanted to do a 'job'. Brannigan apparently told him he did have guns and one of the weapons was later found on Phelan, the one with which he shot at Cunliffe. The allegation against Power was that he received from Phelan an automatic pistol. This also came from Brannigan, along with about 300 rounds of ammunition. Mr Howard Roberts, prosecuting solicitor in the police court, said that it might be found necessary to prefer an even graver charge against Brannigan and Power.

It was announced that the police were seeking the killer whom they had now identified as an Irish-American gunman called John McAteer. At an inquest on 28 June, a jury found that McAteer murdered Thomas Lovelady, aided and abetted by James Phelan. A reward of £50 was offered for information leading to McAteer's arrest.

At the inquest, after hearing evidence and eyewitness accounts of the raid and its aftermath, Deputy Coroner Mills Roberts asked Detective Superintendent Senagles to read out a statement allegedly given to Phelan while in police custody. It stated that Phelan was born at Inchicore in Ireland. Describing the raid, Phelan said he closed the door and stood with his back to it while the other man went behind the counter, the flaps of which were open. There were two girls in the shop and one of them went to the telephone and tried to ring up. The other made a movement as if to go to the back of the shop, but then stood still. According to Phelan:

> The girl at the telephone began to scream. I opened the door and went into Scotland Road. As I turned into Newsham Street I heard a shot and began to run. A little way down I was overtaken by the other man and we were pursued by a crowd. I fired a shot over the man's head and one on the ground to frighten back the crowd. I was then knocked down and arrested.

Phelan then outlined the preparations for the raid. He was living at the time at Thomas Gowland's lodging house in Byrom Street, where he had been since 8 June, three days before the raid. Phelan allegedly said that 'McAteer had a .38 revolver and had been living at North Clarence Street in Dublin. On 11 June, McAteer had said "I will see you at six tonight. Have the guns at Gowland's at six. One of them post offices has got to go up".' Phelan continued:

> I had previously borrowed a .22 automatic pistol from John Brannigan

of the Communist Party. He sent it to me by James Horan, also of the party. I also received some .22 ammunition, a .32 pistol and a .38 revolver with ammunition. So far as I was concerned, the attack on the post office was not prearranged, except for the fact that I concurred when McAteer said one of those post offices had to go up.

Phelan also said:

I never had any intention of shooting anyone, and I did not produce a pistol in the post office until I tried to frighten the crowd. I could easily have shot the man who grappled with me, as I was at point blank range, and could not have missed him if I aimed at him. I did not believe McAteer would shoot at anybody either, but would only use it to frighten people like I did.

A second statement made to Inspector Moore on 14 June, and read out by Mills Roberts, contained more details from Phelan. He had said he wanted to turn king's evidence and allegedly claimed:

In March 1922 I was approached by James Cully and Joseph Kennedy to assist them in a hold-up either at Higgins the butcher's or a post office in Scotland Road, but it was closed. Cully and Kennedy accompanied me. I afterwards backed out, and the matter dropped for some time. McAteer afterwards told me that he also had been approached on the subject by the same men. The matter was revived again last month. On Monday 11 June, McAteer, Power and I walked along Scotland Road, as I was to be shown where the post office was. McAteer was to show me. When we got near the Rotunda, he discovered that we had passed it. We did not turn back, but went along Stanley Road where Power had said there were some banks. Afterwards I met Power and McAteer in St John's Gardens about 1.30 p.m. We walked along Scotland Road as far as Addison Street. We arranged to meet Power at 7 p.m. that night for no particular purpose. When Power was leaving, McAteer said to him: 'Bring that empty gun along'.

About the guns Phelan said:

I wish to add that this gun was one of two sent to me by John Brannigan. On the night, I asked Brannigan for them. I told him that we wanted to do a job. He said they were to be returned unless we had an accident. Power then left us. As McAteer and I crossed the road, I asked him why Power was to bring the gun. He replied: 'One of them post offices has to go up'. He repeated this afterwards when he told me to get the guns from Cully. The .22 automatic pistol which I fetched to 97 Byrom Street on that evening, I had never seen before the evening of 5 June, when I received it with a defective .32 revolver from James Horan.

Phelan said Power did not meet him and McAteer on the night of the raid, as had been arranged.

Phelan, by going with McAteer on the raid, had got himself into very hot water indeed. Summing up the law of murder for the inquest jury, Mr Mills Roberts said: 'If two persons attempt to commit a felony, and in the course of that act one of them, even inadvertently, kills another, the responsibility rests not only upon the one who fires the shot, but upon the other who was there to aid and assist him.'

James Phelan, aged 31, was tried at Manchester for the murder of Thomas Lovelady. Counsel for the prosecution was Mr Madden, defence counsel was Mr Maxwell Fyfe. According to Mr Madden, on the night of the raid the two gunmen had a drink in a nearby pub until a patrolling policeman, who was hanging about, had disappeared. The idea was that one man should ask for a penny stamp and then hold up the cashier.

Referring to the recent activities of Irish Sinn Fein militants since the partition of Ireland some eighteen months earlier, Mr Madden told the jury: 'The prisoner is an Irishman, but that has no effect whatever on this case, for it is not a question of a thing being down in furtherance of a national objective. This was a common murder committed by desperation.'

He continued: 'The prisoner's was not the hand that fired the fatal shot. Not withstanding that, the English law had long held out that where two or three or more set out for the commission of a felonious act, and murder is committed, all are equally guilty.'

For the defence, Mr Fyfe called no evidence, but submitted that there was nothing to show that Phelan had made any agreement to use firearms, nor was he aware that his companion intended to do so. Mr Fyfe said, 'When he left his companion in the post office, he was from that moment acting separately'.

After thirty minutes the jury returned a guilty verdict. Mr Justice

Branson sentenced Phelan to death. As Phelan left the dock for the cells, a distinct sob was heard in the courtroom.

On Friday 27 July, before the Lord Chief Justice and two other judges at the Court of Criminal Appeal, Phelan, represented by Maxwell Fyfe, appealed against his conviction for murder on the ground that he had acted independently of McAteer. Mr Fyfe said that 'After Phelan had escaped, McAteer fired at Lovelady and Lovelady later died. Phelan was chased and caught. During the chase he fired his revolver to frighten his pursuer, but no one was hurt, and the bullets found in Phelan's revolver were not of the same calibre as the lead found in Lovelady's body. McAteer escaped and was still at large.'

Mr Fyfe submitted that the doctrine of common purpose did not extend to render Phelan guilty on these facts. He said, 'There was no evidence that Phelan contemplated that death would result from the enterprise. When Phelan escaped, his responsibility ended for what McAteer did.'

The Lord Chief Justice, giving judgement, said that the question of how the two revolvers came into the possession of Phelan and McAteer was clearly answered by Phelan in a statement he made to the police.

> There was ample evidence on which the jury could find that Phelan went to the office armed for the felonious purpose of robbery and, if need be, of using firearms up to the point of killing to accomplish their purpose or of making good their escape.

The learned judge concluded:

> Mr Justice Branson put the facts fully and clearly before the jury, and he explained to them in unexceptional terms the law applicable to the matter. In these circumstances, there is no ground on which the court can quash the conviction.

On 10 August, a man called Samuel Maginnis, who had been arrested at Dromore, Co. Down, on suspicion of involvement in the robbery, was released from Belfast Gaol, but exhaustive inquires failed to connect him with the crime. On the same day, James Phelan's death sentence was commuted to penal servitude for life. James McAteer was never traced.

Outrage Unsolved

Even at the tender age of eleven, Nellie Clarke was no stranger to tragedy. Her father had been killed in the Great War, one of her sisters died of a fever, another sister was killed in a road accident near her home. In January 1925, Nellie lived with her mother and stepfather at 16 Byrne Avenue in Rock Ferry, one of the corporation houses opposite the entrance of Egerton Park, off Old Chester Road. Nellie's stepfather was Peter Carr, a sheet metalworker and her mother's name was Sarah.

On Saturday 10 January 1925, Nellie went with her brother John to Birkenhead Town Hall. A New Year's entertainment was being given by the mayor to some six hundred war orphans. Mrs Carr, however, was unable to accompany her children to the show.

Nellie enjoyed herself that winter Saturday afternoon. She was given toys, including a doll which she promptly christened Betty. The two children walked back home to Rock Ferry. Nellie was particularly attached

to her new doll during the walk, while John played a mouth organ which he had received. On reaching home, the children were in high spirits and spoke of the happy time they had enjoyed that day. They shared oranges and apples with the rest of the family.

Nellie and John arrived home just before 7 p.m. At about 7.45, Mrs Carr sent Nellie with a message to a second hand dealer's shop at 201 Old Chester Road. The shop was only a few minutes walk away from

Byrne Avenue so when Nellie had not come back home by 9.30 p.m., Sarah Carr went to the shop to make inquiries.

The woman shopkeeper told Mrs Carr that Nellie had indeed been there. She had stayed for only a minute or so and had then left. Returning home, Mrs Carr told her husband and they searched the neighbourhood for the girl, without finding any trace of her. Towards midnight, Mr and Mrs Carr called at Meadow Lane police station in Rock Ferry and reported Nellie missing. By the following morning, a description of the missing girl was circulated to all the constables on duty.

At 8.25 a.m. on the Sunday morning a man called Martin Doran, a painter and decorator who lived at 1 Highfield Grove in Rock Ferry, opened the door leading from the yard into the passage running between Highfield Grove and Spenser Avenue. He let out his two dogs, a large retriever and a spaniel, so that they could have their early morning run. Mr Doran was horrified to see the body of a girl behind a telegraph pole near the door. The child was in a sitting position, leaning slightly to one side, with her head between the pole and the wall. It was clear that she was dead.

Mr Doran sent for the police and body was removed to the Children's Hospital in Woodchurch Road., where it was examined by police surgeon Dr Pierce and by Dr Christian Walsh, the resident doctor. They found that the girl had been raped. There was severe bruising on her neck and wrists. Mr Carr identified the body as that of his stepdaughter Nellie Clarke and she was taken to the mortuary in Price Street.

Chief Constable Captain A. C. Dawson, his deputy, Superintendent A. Lodge, and Detective Inspector Gordon Hughes, were informed of the tragedy and made a close examination of the area near where the body had been found. The place was in the opposite direction to that which Nellie would have taken to the shop. The passage, paved with granite setts, revealed no sign of a struggle. The alleyway was unlit, leading from Spenser Avenue, and then sharply leftwards between the back of houses in Spenser Avenue and those in Highfield Grove, to the rear of Highfield Crescent.

When Nellie left home on the Saturday night, her boots were clean, but when she was found they were muddy. This led to the belief that she had crossed wasteland. There was a plot of spongy open ground fronting Highfield Crescent, which lay between where the body was found and the girl's home.

Police issued a description of the girl in an effort to trace her movements. When she left home on her fatal errand, Nellie wore a light brown cloth coat with a dark fur collar, a red tam o' shanter without a tassel and a red and white striped frock. She wore rather heavy black laced boots. Nellie was described as a bright and clever girl, rather tall for her age, with blue eyes and a cheerful disposition. Her fair hair had been bobbed, but later had been allowed to grow down the middle of her neck. She attended the Ionic Street Council School.

Mr Doran's two dogs had given no warning during the night of any unusual sound near their kennel. Although the dogs had been trained not to react to people passing along the street, Mr Doran was certain that they would bark should anyone touch the yard door. Mr Doran, who slept in the back bedroom, was not disturbed in the night. He told reporters: 'The girl was in a sitting position behind the telegraph pole where she would not be seen by people passing along Spenser Avenue.' He also said that 'The girl's clothing was not disarranged but her features had an agonised look'.

On Monday 12th it was revealed that Scotland Yard officers had detained a man in London on his arrival from Liverpool. This man, however, satisfied the police that he had nothing to do with the murder.

A pair of men's socks were found on the waste ground behind Highfield Grove. A bone button, measuring an inch across, was missing from Nellie's coat. The police theory that the outrage was committed in a sheltered dry place, owing to the clean state of the girl's clothes, could have been verified had the missing button been found. It was now believed that Nellie had been alive at 9.45 p.m., as she was seen at that time in St Paul's Road. Police were asking two people to come forward who, it was believed, saw the girl walking with a man between 8 p.m. and 10 p.m.

Police bloodhounds in the district created a sensation on the Monday afternoon and hundreds of people followed the animals in their searches. One of the dogs, belonging to a Mr McQuilliam from Liverpool, was taken to the telegraph pole in the passage behind Spenser Avenue. After sniffing one of the girl's boots and her stockings, the animal led its owner along the short length of passage into Spenser Avenue, and then up the avenue to the wasteland fronting the Crescent.

The dog spent some time going over the ground before unearthing a bead necklace which had nothing to do with the crime. From there the intrepid beast bolted over a low wall into some allotments and then came

into the street. Followed by the crowd, the dog led Mr McQuilliam round
the Congregational Church into Highfield South. When it dragged its
owner into a field the search was finally given up as unsuccessful.

Hundreds visited the entry where the body was found and as is usual
in such cases, numerous theories and rumours gained ground. Mrs Green
of 88 Spenser Avenue said she heard a sudden wild knocking on her front
door between 9.30 p.m. and 10 p.m. A cry of 'Oh save me, save me!' was
heard in a girl's voice. Nobody, however, could be seen at the door. A Mr
Tudor, who lived a few yards from where the body was found, suggested
that the crime was committed in a motor car. At about 1 a.m. he heard
a car driven into the avenue with its engine running for a few minutes.
Someone got out of the car but no one was heard speaking. Soon the car
was driven off with its gears grating in the stillness of the night.

The Birkenhead police called in the help of the Liverpool detective
department and a reward of £200 was offered for information leading
to the arrest of the killer. An inquest was opened so that evidence of
discovery and identification could be heard, thereby allowing the body to
be released for burial.

Coroner Cecil Holden opened the inquest by declaring, 'She had been
brutally treated and brutally murdered'. The only evidence taken was that
of the stepfather and of Martin Doran, who found the body. The jury
then visited the place where the girl was found. Mr Doran laid down a
mackintosh spread on the ground to illustrate the position of the body.
The jury, with Mr Carr, went by charabanc first to the mortuary and then
to the body scene.

Mr Doran pointed out that the body was found lying on its right side
with the right shoulder leaning against the telegraph pole and the head
bent forward in the space between the pole and the wall. The girl's tam o'
shanter had fallen off and her knees were bent. She had apparently been
carried by the shoulder and back and laid in the position where she was
found. One spot of blood, about the size of a half crown, was found on the
path. There was no sign of a struggle.

The jury visited the house of Mrs Green, who said she heard knocks
and a child crying out for help. She said a fanlight had been lit up above
her front door which may have attracted the girl's attention. Mrs Green's
house directly faced a piece of waste ground so this may have been the
scene of the crime.

Mr Carr gave evidence of identification. He said that Nellie was the daughter of the late John Wallace Clarke, a sheet ironworker. During the war, Mr Clarke was a private in the Highland Light Infantry and had been killed in France. Mr and Mrs Carr had searched through the night for the lost girl. At 8.50 a.m., Detective Inspector Hughes told Mr Carr the body had been found.

A rumour reached the press that an anonymous letter, written on pink paper and posted in Manchester on 13 January, had been received by the Birkenhead Chief Constable, Captain Dawson. It was said that the letter was from one of a courting couple who had stood against a wall in the death passage off Spenser Avenue. The Birkenhead police put out a statement in which they said that this anonymous letter had never existed.

The mayor of Birkenhead, Mrs Mary Mercer, launched a fund to help the bereaved family with their funeral expenses. She said she hoped it would be possible to send Mrs Carr away to her sister's home in the country in order to save her from a possible nervous breakdown. This was because Nellie's death closely followed the loss of another two children. Efforts were being made by the corporation to obtain for the Carr family a house on the Hoylake Road at the north end of the town, in order to remove them from the scene of their latest tragedy.

The funeral of Nellie Clarke took place on the morning of 15 January at Bebington Cemetery. Although the early time of 9 a.m. was kept secret, when the hearse and two cars drove into Byrne Avenue, a crowd quickly assembled. Because the avenue was a short cut for people going to the railway station, many commuters on their way to work stopped to witness the event. The coffin bore five floral tributes, including a wreath from the mayor and another inscribed: 'With Deepest Sympathy from a Schoolmate, A. Foreshaw.'

On Monday 19 January, the police announced that they were making inquiries about a man who got onto a corporation bus on the night of the crime. Tall and well dressed, the man behaved in a very odd manner. He played nervously with a piece of paper and kept laughing hysterically.

Although nothing more was to be heard about this latest suspect, a Mr Mercer, who ran Milne's butcher's shop in New Chester Road, said he saw a man with a little girl pass his shop shortly before 9 p.m. on the fatal night. Mr Mercer did not see clearly the man's face, but he was struck by the uncanny disparity between the couple. They seemed so totally out of place with each other. Turning to his shopboy, Mr Mercer had said: 'He looks like a child-stealer. I bet he is not the child's father.'

A further possible sighting of the girl came to light on the 19th. Nellie had reportedly been seen in several streets not far from her home. Then the missing button from her coat was found on the railway bridge in Rock Lane West. A woman who had crossed from Liverpool to Rock Ferry by the 8.40 p.m. boat was walking home along Rock Lane when she noticed a man and woman talking by the Rock Hotel. As the woman approached, the man left the woman and went towards New Chester Road. As he reached Mersey Road South he was met by a little girl wearing a red tam o' shanter and similar clothes to the dead girl. The girl said to the man, 'You said ten past nine'. The man replied, 'I have come. What are you grumbling about?' He was wearing a dark overcoat which hung closely to his waist. His trousers, she noticed, were well braced up.

By the second week after the murder, the police inquiry already seemed to be completely deadlocked. Following a request by the Birkenhead Watch Committee, help was obtained from the CID Special Branch at Scotland Yard. On 23 January, Chief Inspector Savage and Sergeant Sprackling travelled to Birkenhead from the capital to help solve the crime.

The inquest was resumed on 5 February. When the girl's body was discovered, a woollen vest and a pink-bordered white handkerchief were missing, as well as the coat button found later on the railway bridge. The police were still unable to locate the scene of the crime. Some light, however, was thrown upon the child's movements after she left 16 Byrne Avenue at about 7.45 p.m.

The girl arrived at the second hand shop at about 7.55 p.m. and left again almost at once. At about 8.30 p.m. she was seen by a Mrs Dalton, looking into a sweet shop window in Old Chester Road. Mrs Dalton gave her a penny. A girl friend called Lilian May Smith saw Nellie in Wycliffe Street, near Bedford road, between 8.30 p.m. and 9 p.m., 'skipping along the road and evidently happy'. After the sighting at Mersey Road South, all trace of the child was lost.

Herbert Davies, the Public Analyst, believed that Nellie may have eaten a meal which she had not been given at home. Mr Davies said that there were about eight ounces of undigested food in the dead girl's stomach. This, he said, consisted of apples, oranges, raisins, currants, cake, bread and tea. This, he believed, was unlikely to have been the meal taken much earlier in the day at the town hall.

Police surgeon W. A. Pierce summarised the forensic evidence. There were numerous bruises on the body and severe violence must have been used to have caused the bruises on her right shoulder. These, said Dr Pierce, could have been caused by the girl being thrown violently against an object like a table. The only actual wound in the body was one 3/8 inch long and 1/16 inch deep on the second finger of the right hand. This may have been caused by a ring on the assailant's hand. There was an internal injury to the head, due to a blow or fall which would have caused unconsciousness for about half an hour. Dr Pierce believed that the girl had eaten another meal after she left the town hall. He said that the girl had probably been attacked indoors and had then been carried to the spot where her body was found. Death, said Dr Pierce, was due to shock and exhaustion.

After fifteen minutes, the inquest jury recorded a verdict of 'Wilful murder against some person or persons unknown'.

Coroner Holden completed proceedings by saying, 'The closing of this inquest does not mean that the investigation of the police will be in any way curtailed. On the contrary, they will proceed with continued energy, and I have high hopes indeed that the man who committed the crime will in the near future be brought to judgement.'

More than five years later, hopes of a solution to the crime were raised when, on 18 October 1930, a shabbily dressed Liverpool house painter called Peter Williams, 26, walked into a Chesterfield police station and confessed to the killing. He was put before a magistrate and remanded in custody. But later that day, messages from the Birkenhead police indicated that they were satisfied that Williams was not in the town at the time of the murder. Williams, from Anfield, was thus discharged from custody. However, he was later re-arrested and sent to Walton Prison. After a two-day hearing at the Liverpool police court, the Director of Public Prosecutions offered no evidence and Williams was again set free.

The Nellie Clarke case was never officially closed. The police file remained open, its papers gathering dust and yellowing with age as the years passed by.

Triple Murder

In 1925 there lived at 122 Price Street in Birkenhead, with his wife and three children, a 53-year-old Chinese man by the name of Lock Ah Tam. Born in Canton, Mr Tam was a naturalised British subject who spoke fluent English and had lived in Birkenhead for many years. Regarded as a respectable man of substance, he was the British agent for the shipping firm of Jack A Tai and Co. Ltd.

Mr Tam had arrived in Liverpool from China some thirty years previously. He was then working as a ship's steward and he later went to Barry Dock as a boarding house keeper, and then to Cardiff where in 1905 he married 21-year-old Catherine Morgan.

The Tams came to Birkenhead in 1908 and by 1925 Mr Tam had become one of the best-known Chinese men in the country. He was employed by the Ocean Steamship Company as the superintendent of the Chinese seamen employed by that company. He was a member of several Chinese social organisations as well as being president of the Chinese Republic Progress Club based at Pitt Street in Liverpool's Chinatown.

In view of later events, it is necessary to point out that in June 1924 Lock Ah Tam was declared bankrupt, with a financial loss of £10,000. Possibly as a result of this personal disaster, he had begun to drink heavily. Frequently irritable and excitable, at these times his wife and children had to approach him with great care in case he should lose his temper. He was no longer a man with whom it was easy to live.

The son, Lock Ling Tam, came of age on 1 December 1925. A party was held at Price Street to honour the occasion. About a dozen people were invited. The whole Tam family were there, including Mrs Tam, Cecilia (17) and Doris (19), as well as a young woman called Margaret Sing, whom Mrs Tam treated as her daughter. Lock Ling Tam had only recently returned from a business tour of China.

The Tams had taken Margaret Sing into their family some five years earlier. Her mother had died in 1914 and her father five years later. On the party night of 1 December, Margaret returned home from a visit to

Liverpool at 10.50 p.m. and joined the celebrations. At about 12.45 a.m. the party broke up and Margaret, with Doris and Cecilia, went to bed.

Margaret slept in a bedroom at the top of the house, with Doris. Cecilia occupied a bed in the same room. They were all just getting to sleep when Margaret heard Mr Tam's voice booming out loudly from the floor below. Doris got out of bed, put a coat over her night-dress, and went downstairs. A little later Cecilia got up and went down as well. After a few minutes more, Mr Tam called up to Margaret and told her to get his boots. After fetching them, she returned to the bedroom to get dressed.

Meanwhile, the son, Lock Ling Tam, was awakened by hearing his mother and father shouting. He did not know what they were quarrelling about, but he thought his mother was being knocked about, so he got up. Doris was on the landing and they were soon joined by Cecilia.

The three children went to the bedroom where their father was stamping about and shouting at their mother. Terrified, Ling asked his mother and the girls to go with him next door, to the house of neighbour Mrs Chin. They refused, so Ling went and knocked on Mrs Chin's door. She let him bed down for the night on her sofa. Anxious and afraid for his mother and his sisters in the wake of his father's terrible anger, Ling could get no sleep.

After Margaret Sing had got dressed in her bedroom, she went downstairs to see Doris and Cecilia. As she passed Mr Tam's bedroom, the door was ajar. Looking in, Margaret was able to see, in his reflection in a mirror, Mr Tam standing with a gun or revolver in his hand.

Frightened out of her wits, Margaret ran all the way downstairs and into the sitting room, where she found Mrs Tam and the two girls. Margaret told her breathlessly, 'I have just seen Mr Tam with a gun!' The four terrified women, unable to keep Mr Tam away from them by locking the sitting room door against him, barricaded the door with heavy furniture. Very soon, Mr Tam was hammering on the door and shouting to be let in. The women let out a volley of terrified screaming. The awful noise could be heard by Ling and Mr Chin next door.

Hearing the screams, Ling rushed back to his own house. As Ling looked in at the window, he saw his father with a gun in his hand. He used a flowerpot to break the back kitchen window and climbed in. Then he opened the door for Mrs Chin to enter.

As soon as Mrs Chin had got into the back kitchen, Cecilia, Doris and Margaret Sing came running into the tiny room, having fled from the sitting room when they thought the coast was clear. As Mrs Chin looked out of the room towards the passage, she could see Mrs Tam coming towards her. When Mrs Tam was near the door, a gun was fired. Mrs Tam fell headfirst into the kitchen. Dumbstruck, Mrs Chin looked up at the door and saw two black barrels of a shotgun being poked around it. She closed her eyes, waiting for death. Another shot rang out and Cecilia fell. Doris cried out, 'Daddy, what did you do that for?' With eyes bulging out of his head and frothing at the mouth, Lock Ah Tam fired a revolver twice, into the unprotected form of his young daughter.

Apparently satisfied with his work, Lock Ah Tam moved away from the carnage in the back kitchen, went into his office, and closed the door behind him. Maggie Sing and Mrs Chin fled through the back door screaming 'Murder! Murder!' The son, Lock Ling Tam, ran pell-mell to the Watson Street bridewell to summon police assistance. However, before he got there, Mr Tam had himself calmly announced the terrible news over the telephone to the Central Police Station.

First on the crime scene were Sergeant Hamer and Sergeant Langford, called to the house by young Ling. When they got there the back and front doors were locked. Hamer knocked several times. Getting no answer, he went round to the back of the premises and climbed on to the wall. From this vantage point, Hamer saw Mr Tam in the yard. Hamer asked Tam to open the door and he replied 'Come round to the front'. The Chinese man opened the front door for the two policemen to go inside.

Mr Tam led the sergeant into the sitting room. Hamer asked him what was the matter, to which Tam replied, 'Shot my wife'. Hamer told Tam to be careful of what he said. Pointing to the kitchen, Tam said, 'I have shot my wife and daughter; they are in the back place'. In the back kitchen, Mrs Tam was lying dead in a pool of blood. The dead body of Cecilia was also on the floor. Doris lay unconscious in a sitting position behind the back kitchen door. All three were removed to hospital.

Sergeant Hamer arrested Lock Ah Tam who, on the way to the bridewell, was reported to have said: 'The trouble is through my son. My wife has not a kind word for me. My son is the cause of it all.' When charged, Tam replied, 'Nothing at present'. Doris, although critically injured, gave a deposition to the police from her hospital bed. When Tam reached the bridewell he seemed, according to Sergeant Hamer, to be 'perfectly sober, but slightly agitated'.

Lock Ah Tam appeared in the police court later on the fatal morning, charged with the murder of his wife Catherine and his daughter Cecilia Ruth, together with the attempted murder of his younger daughter Doris. He was remanded in custody.

On 22 December an inquest was conducted by Borough Coroner Cecil Holden. Doris Tam was still in hospital. The events of the dreadful night were recounted. Mr Kwok Tsan Chin, the Tams' next door neighbour, told the court that he was a business associate of Mr Tam who, said Kwok, regularly drank considerable quantities of whisky. After the shooting, Tam said to him, in Chinese, 'I am in trouble. You look after the business and do your best. If I get hung, get my body out and bury me by my wife and daughters'.

Coroner Holden, from the bench, warned the inquest jury that the question of Tam's mental condition did not concern them. He declared: 'This is infinitely the worst case I have met in my experience as a coroner. Frankly, I cannot understand the reason for Mr Tam's actions. I have known him for a considerable time.' Unsurprisingly, the jury's verdict was 'Wilful murder against Lock Ah Tam'.

At another police court hearing on 23 December, Mr A. C. Shepherd, the prosecuting solicitor, said that the mother's 'outspoken affection for her son could have been the motive for the alleged crime'. Mr Shepherd also said that 'Not the least peculiar feature of the case is the undoubted respectability of the accused man. There is no more respectable personality among the Chinese community on Merseyside'.

During the supper before the party at Price Street, the son's health was toasted by his father, who wished him success in his future. During the dancing, father and mother danced together. Mrs Tam said she would like to see her son grow up to be as good as his father. The whole assembly stood up during the drinking of the toast. Such was the apparent conviviality and friendliness within the family before it was rent asunder by Tam's terrifying violence.

Doris Ah Tam spent Christmas and New Year in her bed at the Borough Hospital. She had been shot by a revolver; Mrs Tam and Cecilia had been killed by a sporting gun. Doris had a circular wound on her cheek, opposite the left ear. There was also another small wound on the same side of her face under the middle of the lower jaw caused by two revolver bullets. On 11 December a piece of lead had been removed from

Sir Edward Marshall-Hall KC

Born Brighton 1858 (died February 1929), Marshall-Hall was to became a famous barrister. The son of doctor, from whom he acquired a knowledge of medicine, he attended Rugby School for two years then became a clerk at a tea merchant's, from which he acquired an insight into the business world. Some travelling also built up a body of knowledge of the world that would aid him as an advocate.

He was sent by his father to St John's College, Cambridge, in 1880, taking a pass degree in 1882, and he was called to the bar in 1888.

Marshall-Hall's looks and personality were a major assets in his career and ones he made the most of. He was handsome and had a commanding presence that appealed to solicitors and lay clients. He became known as the Great Defender because of his abilities in representing alleged murderers. Although he did not practice regularly in the criminal courts, the publicity generated by the cases he was involved in kept him in the public eye. He built up successful law firm but fell into serious financial difficulties as result of the libel action in 1901 against the *Daily Mail*, though he recovered and rebuilt his practice again. In 1906 he was elected as MP for Southport for the Conservatives, a seat he held until 1906. Between 1910 and 1916 he represented the Liverpool constituency of East Toxteth, but he was not as successful as an MP than as a barrister. In the *Dictionary of National Biography* he is recalled thus:

> Marshall-Hall had been a unique figure. If his reputation was more public than professional, at his best he was a powerful advocate, and always the kindest and most generous of leaders. In many ways there was much of the child in him. He had a passion for showing off, tempered by an attractive simplicity and combined with a love of the marvellous, which made him on questions of fact somewhat of an impressionist. But there was about his personality something which even his most austere critics found hard to resist.

the wound in the skull and X-ray examinations revealed that there were still two pieces of lead in Doris's head. On 22 January, after lingering in Hospital for fifty-one days, Doris died. Lock Ah Tam would now face trial for three murders.

The trial of Lock Ah Tam for triple murder opened at Chester Assizes on Friday 5 February 1926, before Mr Justice McKinnon and a jury. Prosecuting counsel was Sir Ellis Griffith KC. Acting for the defence was star barrister Sir Edward Marshall-Hall KC. Such was the public interest in the case that for hours a long queue of people stood up in the rain waiting to be admitted to the court.

The accused man pleaded not guilty. The case for the prosecution was overwhelming. In an attempt to nullify it, Marshall-Hall put forward a defence of insanity fuelled by alcohol.

During the course of the prosecution's evidence, George Youd, a friend of Tam, was cross-examined by Marshall-Hall. Youd said that he left the party at 9.45 p.m. when 'everything was most pleasant'. At the party, champagne and whisky were consumed and before the party he and Tam had 'a couple of beers each' at the Westminster Hotel. Youd said that since his bankruptcy, Tam had been 'a different man' and 'took a great deal more drink' than before. When he had a few drinks he was 'like a lunatic'.

George Youd told the court that Tam had, in 1918, sustained severe head injuries when he was struck by a billiard cue wielded by a Russian sailor. The marks of this attack, said Youd, were visible on Tam's head. Youd also gave evidence about an incident some six months before in a hotel. Someone contradicted Tam who picked up a glass and smashed it down on the table. Youd said that he was himself struck by a sliver of glass. He had noticed that Tam 'became excited on the slightest provocation but then subsided again very quickly'.

Lock Ling Tam, in cross-examination by Marshall-Hall, said that when drunk his father was 'out of the ordinary and got funny ideas'.

'Did not the sight of your father absolutely terrify you?'

'Yes', replied the son, 'but he has been a good father to me.'

'Had you any doubt that your father was going mad?'

'My mother talked to me about it,' replied Ling.

On the Saturday, the second day of the trail, the case for the defence was opened by Sir Edward Marshall-Hall. Chinese men in different parts of the world had subscribed to a fund approaching the huge amount of

£1,000, towards Tam's legal expenses. As a result of this generosity, Tam had been able to engage probably the most famous and most successful defence counsel at the English criminal bar.

In his opening remarks to the jury, Marshall-Hall said:

> There is not a shadow of a doubt that three people died as a result of injuries inflicted by the Chinaman in the dock, that the wife was shot with one charge from a double-barrelled gun, Cecilia with the charge from the second barrel, and that Doris was killed by a bullet or bullets from a revolver. If you were to search all the Greek tragedies you would not find one more poignant than that.

The defence to murder was, said Marshall-Hall,

> a latent condition of disease brought into active conditions by the taking of drink by the prisoner. Although he was not incapacitated by the drink, it acted as a lever to bring the latent disease to the surface, and the act was performed in that condition of the disease. The causation of it was the mixture of drink and disease.

The burden of proof of insanity lay upon the defence. Detective Chief Inspector Burgess gave evidence that Tam was, as George Youd had mentioned, knocked on the head in the Chinese Republican Progress Club. It was with a billiard cue used by two drunken Russian sailors. Latterly, said Burgess, Tam had been affected by the attack. He estimated that Tam drank '1½ to 2 bottles of whisky a day'.

Dr Ernest Reeve, medical superintendent at Rainhill Mental Hospital, said the blow on the head which Tam had received in 1918 'might lead to a gradual deterioration of the mental and moral character, craving for alcohol, and epilepsy'. Dr Reeve also said, 'The more I hear of the crime the more I am drawn to the conclusion that Mr Ah Tam was in a condition of epileptic automatism'.

To refute the claim of insanity, Sir Ellis Griffith called two witnesses. The first witness was Dr Ahern of Walton Prison. He said that when admitted to prison, Tam was 'mentally cool and gave no sign of abnormality'. There was no evidence, he said, 'of the underlying bone having been affected by the blow received some years ago'. Only once, said Dr Ahern, had Tam shown a sign of mental disorder. He had no evidence whatever that Tam was an epileptic or was mentally unsound.

Dr Watson of Brixton Prison, who had also examined Tam, said, 'There was nothing to suggest that Ah Tam was not rational. I can hardly imagine how anyone can hold the theory that the accused had an epileptic seizure at the time of the crime'. Watson also said: 'The whole evidence suggests to me that the condition of the accused was alcoholic and not epileptic'.

It was up to the jury alone to decide that Tam was out of his mind when he shot his family. They would have to be convinced that Tam did not realise the nature and quality of his actions because of a disease of the mind.

In his final speech to the jury, Marshall-Hall pointed out that there was an entire absence of motive as far as the two girls were concerned, but there was the question of a quarrel with the mother. 'Without rhyme or reason the man shot those he loved most.' The defence counsel said: 'Is not the real difficulty, putting aside the medical evidence, how could any sane man believe that another sane man could commit such a crime? Was it not the act of a man whose reason, in the words of Lord Coleridge, was dethroned?'

After Mr Justice McKinnon had summed up the evidence and briefed the jury on the law of insanity, the jury retired to consider their verdict. After only twelve minutes they brought in a verdict of guilty.

When sentence of death was being passed upon him, Lock Ah Tam, short and stout with a dark moustache, stood with his head slightly bent and did not once look at the judge. With some signs of bewilderment, he turned when a warder touched him on the shoulder, and walked down out of the dock.

An appeal against Tam's death sentence was lodged on 13 February and heard at the Court of Criminal Appeal on 8 March before a tribunal of Lord Chief Justice Hewart, Mr Justice Avory and Mr Justice Finlay.

Sir Edward Marshall-Hall, arguing his appeal, said that the real defence to the charge was the crime itself. 'In the whole of my career I have never known of a case of such a tragic nature.' The grounds of the appeal, he said, were entirely based on the summing up of Mr Justice McKinnon.

He had apparently been under the apprehension that the only defence put forward was that of insanity. There was however the defence that at the time of the commission of the crime, Ah Tam was so under the influence of drink as to be unable to form a felonious intention. The evidence which supported the latter defence ought to have been left to the jury, but it was ignored.

Turning to the insanity element in his appeal, Marshall-Hall continued:

> There was medical evidence that Ah Tam was suffering from epileptic automatism which caused a craving for drink. No reasonable explanation of the crime exists except on the basis that Ah Tam's reason was dethroned.

His crime, said Hall, was that of 'a hitherto respectable citizen who had killed the three persons whom he most loved'.

Giving judgement, Lord Hewart said that it was remarkable that the three charges of murder made against Ah Tam had been included in one indictment. He pointed out that in an indictment for murder, only one charge of murder should be made, nor should a charge of any other crime be included. 'No injustice', said Hewart, 'appears to have resulted and the defence has made no complaint.' He further maintained:

> The defence of drunkenness, such as it was, was not withdrawn from the jury at the trial. The judge doubtless criticised the value of that defence, but the matter was put before the jury and, whatever the real weight was attached to it in any quarter, it is impossible to say that the summing-up, when read as a whole, did not fairly put before the jury every consideration that could be taken into account on behalf of the applicant.

Hewart said that when Tam surrendered to the police he spoke naturally, although he was slightly agitated. He took the police into his office and lit a cigarette. The guns were neatly packed away, Tam's safe was locked, and in it was a five-chambered revolver. 'The defence was the usual one,' said Hewart, 'the almost invariable defence of insanity coupled with the question of drink.' As was without doubt expected, the appeal was dismissed.

Lock Ah Tam was hanged at Walton at 8 a.m. on the morning of 23 March. He walked firmly from the condemned cell and met his death bravely. Tam's sister-in-law, Mrs Ralph, handed in a bunch of spring daffodils to be dropped into his grave. In Liverpool's Chinatown, flags flew at half-mast in tribute to a famous son of China.

Birkdale Sandhills

On Tuesday 9 March 1926, a young man by the name of Hector Collingwood Leach walked into Birkdale police station and asked the duty officer if he could have an ambulance. He said: 'There is a woman ill who had taken poison. I have taken some too, but got rid of mine.' When questioned further, Leach said that the girl had lost her job and would not go back either to her parents or to her friends. He could not, he said, see her staying out alone, so they decided to die together by taking poison.

Leach took the police out onto the sandhills at Birkdale, and there they found 18-year-old Elizabeth Haslam, unconscious and barely alive, her body covered in sand. She died some fifteen minutes after arriving at Southport Infirmary.

Elizabeth Haslam and Hector Leach, also 18, had been seeing each other for eighteen months or so. The girl had left her home at Clarendon Street, in the Chorlton district of Manchester, about a year previously. Since then she lived in apartments in Manchester, near to the factory where she worked as a clothier's machinist. Leach, who lived in Canning Street, Hulme, worked in a rubber factory.

When told that he might be charged with murder and attempted suicide, Leach said Elizabeth had quarrelled with her parents and had lost her job. She had, he said, threatened previously to 'put an end to herself'. Leach said that on Monday he had bought some Lysol disinfectant which they both had taken to kill themselves.

On 10 March, Leach appeared at the Southport Police Court, charged with murder and with attempted suicide. He was remanded in custody for a week, and then for a further three days at a second hearing. His next appearance was at a committal hearing on Saturday 20 March.

At the committal, Detective Superintendent Wignall produced letters from the girl to Leach, whom she called 'my dearest boy'. One letter concluded: 'Darling, we will both end together and that is what you have always wanted – Your broken hearted sweetheart, Lizzie.' It began to look as if, following her parents' disapproval of their relationship, the couple had made some kind of suicide pact.

Dr Hubert Lawson of Southport Infirmary stated that the girl had died from Lysol poisoning. On the same day, the doctor examined Leach and found he had the symptoms of 'suffering the effects of an irritant poison'. In Leach's favour was Dr Lawson's admission that Elizabeth, having been out in the open during the whole of the two previous nights, would have been much weakened, and this would have speeded up her death.

After the prosecution case had been heard, the defence solicitor, Mr Compton Carr, took the unusual course of presenting a defence case to the magistrates. Normally, the defence would have been reserved for the later trial by jury.

Mr Carr submitted that there was no evidence of a common agreement between the couple that the accused should destroy the girl and himself. 'It was the girl's desire and her's alone that she should take poison.' Mr Carr then called on Hector Leach to give evidence in his own defence.

Leach testified that he first met the girl in a dance hall about fifteen months before. She was, he said, 'very strong-willed and difficult to advise'. About a month previously she told him he was very jealous and they should agree to stop going about together. However, within a day or two they made up their differences. Just after Christmas, the girl threatened to go away and drown herself, and he told her 'not to be silly'. On the Saturday before her death they went dancing together, and then Elizabeth refused to go home or to her lodgings. She wanted Leach to leave her to wander about by herself but he refused. Then they walked about the streets all the Saturday night, sheltering in doorways from the rain.

Continuing his evidence, Leach described how, on the Sunday night, the girl said she was going to 'walk about and end herself', so he stopped with her and they slept in a field. On the Monday they got a train to Southport, where the girl, said Leach, 'threatened to throw herself into the marine lake'. Leach said he told her the water was cold, whereupon she told him, 'There are more means than one'.

According to Leach, Elizabeth asked him to buy her some sweets and some poison, so he bought some Lysol. Leach said: 'I had no desire to do away with myself, but I saw it was useless arguing with her. The matter had got so much on my nerves during the three days and three nights, so much that I thought I would end myself.'

On the Monday evening, said Leach, they walked to the sandhills, where they stayed all night. He said he tried to persuade her to return home, but she refused. 'I told her that if she would not change her mind, I would do away with myself as well. She told me not to.' Leach was awake, smoking all night on the sandhills, while the girl slept.

At 6 a.m. the girl awoke. She said she had better take the Lysol because 'I don't want people to see me on the sands'.

'She then scribbled a note to her mother,' said Leach, 'and drank the Lysol'. Although Leach slapped her back to try and make the girl spit out the poison, she passed out at once. Leach said he then took a swig out of the bottle but immediately vomited the liquid back.

Leach testified that shortly after the girl had passed out, he left her lying on the dunes and walked to Birkdale post office to telephone for an ambulance. 'After waiting a quarter of an hour I was told to ring up the police.' He did not know, he said, that the police station was only a few yards from the post office, and so he returned to the girl and tried to revive her. Because he failed in this, he said, he went to the police station and told them what had happened.

Leach declared: 'The reason I said to the police that I suggested it was because I wanted to take the blame. It is not true that it was my idea that we should do it.' When he had said 'We decided to die together by taking poison' it was, said Leach, 'the first thing that came into my mind to say'. Leach was now denying that a suicide pact had ever existed. 'It was', he said, 'under my own influence that I took it, and I did so because she was taking it'.

Under cross examination by prosecuting solicitor Saywell, Leach said

Lysol poisoning

Lysol is a particularly strong poison chemically related to carbolic acid which can blister and burn the skin and cause pain and irritation if swallowed. Like carbolic acid, it is used as a disinfectant and as an ingredient in other cleaning products. Lysol's toxicity was widely known and only a small amount is needed to kill a person, so it was a common choice of poison for a person wishing to commit suicide.

the girl wanted to have a bottle of Lysol and drink the poison, but 'instead of that she emptied her face powder tin. I filled it with Lysol and she drank out of that. I drank from the bottle.' He had kept the disinfectant in his pocket all through the night. Marriage, said Leach had been mentioned between them, but only in fun. He said: 'I was expecting to marry her in three years time or so. She laughed at the idea.'

For the defence, Compton Carr called into the witness box 17-year-old Minnie Kenny, of Buxton Street, Chorlton. She was a workmate of the dead girl. Minnie said that Lizzie used to get leave from her work to go dancing. On one occasion, Lizzie told her about an article she had been reading, about poison. 'We talked about death', said Minnie. They discussed how they would like to die. Minnie said she would rather be drowned. Lizzie maintained that 'Poison is better', and mentioned prussic acid. 'She said she didn't want work and knew what she was going to do.' According to Minnie, 'A fortnight ago Lizzie said she would give me her dance frock and costume, as she would not need them any more'. Minnie now had the costume. She said that on 6 March Lizzie told her that if she did not see her by 4 p.m. on the next afternoon she would never see her again. 'She said she was fed up with everything.'

The Southport magistrates had to decide whether there was a *prima facie* case against Leach. This they did without leaving the room to discuss the matter and Leach was duly committed for trial by jury.

Liverpool Assizes at St George's Hall was the venue for Leach's trial on Monday 26 April 1926. The prosecution witnesses who had testified at the committal hearing again gave evidence. Mrs Elsie Toole, with whom Elizabeth Haslam had lodged in Manchester, said she was a headstrong girl who would not take advice. She had been 'rather morbid with intervals of brightness'. More than once the girl declared she was 'fed up with things'. Often she had spoken of death and once, said Mrs Toole, the girl said she would 'not mind dying'.

The prosecution, led by E. G. Hemmerde KC, was attempting to convince the jury that there had been a suicide pact between the couple, and that this had gone wrong. As the surviving member of the pact, Leach would, in law, be guilty of murder.

For the defence, Mr Maxwell Fyfe objected to the hearing in evidence of three letters written by Leach while awaiting trial in Preston Gaol. Those letters were very damaging to Leach but the judge, Mr Justice

Swift, ruled that they were admissible as evidence. The letters were then read out by the clerk of the court. In one letter, addressed to Lily, the girl's sister, Leach had written:

> Please forgive me for the wrong I have done to you and your family. You know how I loved Lizzie. I thought I should have died with her but the worst happened and I survived. You all thought she was happy but you don't know the little troubles she put up with bravely.

In a letter to his brother Charles, Leach wrote:

> I wonder what you are all thinking of me now. Well Charlie, I have done it now and I am ready to face my punishment. I know that you and Robin will stay with mother and comfort her. Don't worry about me now will you. I have nothing to fear. Whatever happens to me will not be enough to atone for poor Lizzie. I suppose mother is putting this all down to jazzing. Well that is all wrong. Now Charlie, you will look after mother, won't you.

A third letter, to Mrs Toole, ran:

> I suppose you all know about this lot now, and you will be wondering what possessed us to do it. If I had not been so afraid of being called chicken hearted, I should have told you on Saturday night, but I didn't want Lizzie to think me a coward. I have to stand my trial yet, and by then you will know more about it.

Although Leach had given evidence at the committal hearing, Mr Fyfe did not call upon him to testify at the trial. Consequently, Leach was unable to give the jury his version of the events surrounding the girl's death. Mr Fyfe called no evidence at all for the defence and relied totally upon his final address to the jury.

Mr Fyfe suggested to the jury that there was doubt as to whether or not Leach and the girl had agreed to kill themselves. He said: 'The girl, who was of strong will, had a big influence over Leach and she was inclined to have periods of morbidity. I suggest that, far from encouraging the girl to take her life, it is probable he told her he would take Lysol himself as a threat to prevent the girl from doing so.'

In his summing up, Mr Justice Swift told the jury that if two persons agreed to commit suicide, and in consequence of the agreement one died and the other survived, then in law the survivor is guilty of murder.

The jury were out for only fifteen minutes. The verdict was guilty, and the jury foreman added: 'We recommend him to mercy, believing that the dead girl was the leading spirit.' Asked by the judge if he had anything to say why sentence of death should not be passed upon him, Leach drew himself up sharply and replied in a clear voice, 'No sir'. Mr Justice Swift said the recommendation to mercy would be passed to the appropriate quarter and would receive due consideration. The death sentence, automatic in cases of murder, was then pronounced.

At the Court of Criminal Appeal on 20 May 1926 Leach applied for leave to appeal against his conviction. Maxwell Fyfe, for Leach, submitted that it was common ground that Leach was in the girl's company and that he had been with her since the preceding Saturday. Fyfe complained that the judge, in summing up the case, inaccurately directed the jury on the law relating to suicide pact cases. Fyfe said there might be an agreement of such a character as not to constitute the crime of murder in the survivor of the pact. He added:

> An agreement in which the survivor encourages the person who died is one thing; an agreement into which the survivor is forced by the other party is another thing. In the present case Leach was acting under the influence of the girl. It is still a question of doubt whether the survivor of a "pact" who is under the dominance of the party to it who dies is guilty of murder.

The judges considering the application were Lord Hewart, Mr Justice

Suicide and suicide pacts

Most successful suicides are carried out in isolation and have been carefully planned. A lonely place is chosen, or a time when no one is expected, and the means used are carefully worked out. Rates of suicide are three times more common in men as in women and the lowest rates exists amongst the married, with higher rates within the unskilled and professional classes. Doctors and vets, who have access to drugs and the knowledge of how to administer and overdose, have higher than average rates of suicide.

In the cases in this book, poverty and unemployment feature as reasons behind some of the suicide pacts. There is also often a correlation between economic conditions and rates of suicide, as for example during the Depression of 1932–33 when the rate was exceptionally high. It is more prevalent in the city than in the countryside because generally the city dweller has a greater risk of living a dislocated and isolated life, despite the numbers of people around him/her, than in the closer communities of the rural village/town. High rates have been reported in areas that have large numbers of boarding houses with a socially isolated and itinerant clientele. Where an individual has lost their sense of social integration with their community their death is referred to as 'egotistic' suicide. 'Anomic' suicide refers to people who live in a society that is in the midst of major social change and is unsettled, leading to a sense of there being little collective order. The upheavals after the end of the First World War both socially and economically produced the conditions for this sense of alienation. Other factors such as mental illness and substance abuse, e.g. alcoholism, increase the risk for suicide.

Suicide pacts are not common and investigators have to decide whether both participants were intent on dying, or whether one person aides another to commit suicide without wanting to die themselves. There is usually a close relationship between the participants of the pact and the initiator is in most cases a mentally ill man influencing a sane woman.

Salter and Mr Justice Finlay. After leaving court to discuss their findings, they returned and Lord Hewart gave judgement:

> The summing-up might have been more full in its explanation of the law, but the longer it was, the more adverse to Leach it must have been. Whatever might be the fate of other cases, two things were established by overwhelming evidence in the present case. One was that at the critical moment Leach was with the girl; the other was that Leach, the purchaser of the poison, was aiding and abetting her. On the facts it is impossible to say that the summing-up was inadequate. The application if refused.

Two days after the appeal hearing, it was announced that the Home Secretary had advised King George V to respite the sentence of death passed on Leach. His sentence was commuted to imprisonment for life.

Speke Wood

At 7 p.m. on Monday 15 August 1927, farm labourer John Ginnelly was making his way home to Mersey View Farm at Speke after a hard day's work in the fields. As Ginnelly passed the boundary hedge of Dam Wood in Oglet his attention was drawn to a tall man standing behind the hedge. The man, who had a swarthy complexion, was swinging his arms wildly above his head. He kept pointing towards a nearby wood and jumping up and down in an agitated fashion. When Ginnelly reached the arm-swinging man, he could see that he was bleeding from a long cut in his throat.

The man could not speak. Instead, he took out a pencil and scribbled on a card the message, 'Save her, not me'. When Ginnelly reached the farm his master rang for the police.

Constable McLoughlin of the Lancashire County Police, stationed at Speke, drove out in a pony and trap to Dam Lane. The wounded man was sitting on the lane side with blood pouring down from his throat. As McLoughlin approached, the bleeding man waved his hand and pointed towards Dam Wood. He tried to speak but he could not manage to do so because of a severed windpipe.

The man wrote on a Liverpool greyhound coursing card: 'I love her only. We could not live. She is in there. Save her, not me.' The constable tied a cloth around the man's neck and took him in the trap to Garston Hospital.

At the hospital, after the man's wound had been dressed, McLoughlin tried to get more information about the woman from him. The man wrote on a business card: 'The name is in her bag, E. Jennings, 35 Prescot Road, Fairfield. We wanted to die together.' After McLoughlin had formally cautioned the man, he further wrote on the card: 'I cut the woman's throat with a razor. I covered her with her coat as there were thousands of flies about.'

Meanwhile, Inspector Yates and several police officers from Widnes began to search the wood. At about 8 p.m., some 150 yards from the roadway, they found a body of a young woman lying face upwards in bracken behind some thick rhododendron bushes, her head resting upon her handbag. There was a deep gash in her throat and a bloodstained razor lay by her side. The body was removed to Speke mortuary.

The man under treatment at Garston Hospital turned out to be 37-year-old William Maynell Robertson, a salesman, of 10 Channell Road in

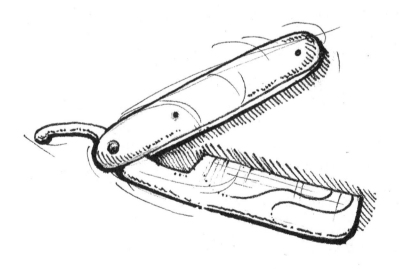

the Kensington district of Liverpool. He was in no fit state to appear in court. Nevertheless, the legal process went ahead quickly with an inquest at Widnes, opened on 17 August by the South West Lancashire coroner, Samuel Brighouse.

The dead woman had been identified as Mary Evelyn Jennings, aged 33. She had been in business as a hairdresser with a shop at 35 Prescot Road. Her brother Thomas, an insurance manager of 34 Kingsley Road in Chester, had identified the body of his sister, whom he had last seen alive about two months earlier.

Mr Jennings said in evidence that on the Monday afternoon he received from his sister a telegram which read: 'Come Prescot Road. Very Urgent – Evelyn'. It had been handed in at Hale village post office at 1.15 p.m. Mr Jennings went over to the shop and saw his mother, who told him that Evelyn had gone out shopping. Her daughter's return was, she said, overdue. Thomas Jennings did not mention the telegram to his mother, but left word with her to tell Evelyn to phone him when she returned.

Thomas rang the shop at 4.30 p.m. and was told that his sister had not yet come home. He then went into Liverpool and arrived at his mother's house at 6.20 p.m. He showed his mother the telegram and, as there was no news of Evelyn by 8 p.m., he contacted the police, ironically about the same time as the body was being discovered in Dam Wood.

Mr Jennings said that at 12.50 p.m. on the Monday he got a message from the Liverpool police, asking him to go to Speke mortuary. On the Tuesday, Mr Jennings received a letter from Evelyn in the morning post. The coroner read it out:

Dear Tom, I find I cannot go on. I love Pat Robinson more than anything. He has rotten health and no luck anyway. He has tried heaven's hard for any kind of job, and to save him going out once before I tried to hang on, thinking surely something would turn up. Nothing has. Now he is going I don't feel that I can possibly hang on without him and my luck is not too good. Things look a bit rotten, but some money will come in very shortly from him which will more than square up and the business can sell. If you keep the shop open, the week's taking will pay wages. I am sending you a wire from Hale, where we are. You will find us in a wood in Boundary Lane off the main road to Liverpool – E.

Dr McCausland, the police surgeon at Widnes, said that Evelyn's fatal wound could not have been self-inflicted, so clearly Robertson would now be facing a murder charge in due course.

Evelyn Jennings used to work as an assistant to the previous owner of the hairdressing business and when he had retired about two years earlier, she took over the business and had recently completed the purchase. By all accounts, the business was flourishing. There was a fully equipped men's saloon and Evelyn had employed two assistants. She supported her widowed mother and was said to be very popular with her customers.

A little over a year earlier, Robertson, whom Miss Jennings knew as 'Pat Robinson', was in partnership with a Mrs Hall in a confectionery business in Prescot Road, just a few doors away from Evelyn's hairdressing shop. Owing to a disastrous fire, the sweet shop closed down, most of the stock having been destroyed in the flames. Robertson continued to live a few blocks away from Evelyn's shop and what had started as a friendship between neighbours in business had apparently developed into a deeper relationship; a tragic one as things turned out.

At Hale on the afternoon of the tragedy, Evelyn Jennings posted two letters, one of which was to her brother Thomas in Chester. The other letter she sent to a lifelong friend, Mrs Tomlinson of Elm Lea in Neston. This second letter read:

> I am going out. Stiffy is going to do it for me and himself as well. There is no luck anywhere for him, try as he will, and I can't help any more. We have had this alternative for weeks, and tried everything, so it seems it must be. I have sent a letter to Tom at Chester, and am wiring him to go to gran. It is a shame to worry anyone, but I cannot sit down beaten all round and he go. Whatever happens, and I know now that I can't exist without him. Anything of mine you want settle with D and see if anyone else wants a bit or just wants to forget. I love you a lot – Eve.

There was a postscript which said: 'Terribly sorry, when you have so much to worry you. Have no guts left. I love you both – Eve.'

Robertson came up at the Widnes Police Court on 12 September. After a short hearing, he was remanded in custody for eight days. On 20 September 1927 committal proceedings opened at Widnes.

According to Dr Croghan, at the Garston Hospital, Robertson had confessed to him that 'I cut the woman's throat with my razor. Before it happened I took off my collar and tie and held her throat up to me, and when I cut her throat she held her arms out to me, and I knelt down beside her'. Robertson also told Croghan to 'find out if Evelyn is all right. She is in the woods. I have told them where she is. They should easily find her. It's no use crying over spilt milk, but it would be some consolation to know she is alive'. He also said: 'She was fed up and wanted to go out. I asked her if she was serious and she replied "Yes".'

Norma Davies of Penny Lane, one of Evelyn's assistants, told the court that Robertson paid almost daily visits to the shop. On the morning of the tragedy she received a phone call from Robertson saying that Miss Jennings would not be home for an hour, but that she was not to tell the woman's mother that he had spoken to her.

David Maxwell-Fyfe

David Maxwell-Fyfe was born in 1900 in Aberdeen, and died in January 1967. After being called to the bar he went to Liverpool to work in the chambers of George Lynsky, later Mr Justice Lynsky. He was MP for West Derby 1935–54, was made Home Secretary 1951–54, then Lord Chancellor 1954–62, and he was the Deputy Chief Prosecutor at the Nuremberg Trials 1945–46. A firm supporter of the death penalty, he refused a reprieve for Derek Bentley.

At the close of the hearing, Robertson pleaded not guilty to the murder charge, adding: 'I have only one thing to say: she is not to blame. I reserve my defence.'

Robertson's trial took place on 28 October 1927 at St George's Hall. In almost inaudible tones he pleaded not guilty and Mr Maxwell Fyfe put forward a defence of insanity. Dr Croghan, of Chapel Road, Garston, said that Robertson had been drinking a bottle of whisky a day, and also reported that Robertson's aunt had died of acute mania, and his mother was neurotic. 'He came', said Dr Croghan, 'from a perfectly respectable home and turned to crime.'

For the prosecution, Dr Ahern of Walton Prison said he had seen 'no evidence of mental unsoundness' during the time Robertson had been in his care. There was nothing to show he was of unsound mind on 15 August. But Mr Maxwell Fyfe was intent on trying to save his client from the gallows by making a case for insanity: 'The jury has the right to infer from Robertson's family history that there is a predisposition towards mental unsoundness.'

In addition, Mr Fyfe cited his client's severe war experience in the East, France and Russia, which would, said Fyfe, 'tend to undermine his physical and mental stamina'. On leaving the army, Robertson failed to find secure permanent work, got short of money, and took to drink and gambling. 'All this,' said the defence counsel, 'produced an awful feeling of hopelessness which apparently was shared by the woman with whom he had become friendly.' Mr Fyfe submitted that 'at the moment of the tragedy, Robertson would have been entirely unable to pass a rational judgement on the moral quality of the act'. In other words, Fyfe was saying that Robertson would not have known that what he was doing was a criminal offence.

The judge, Mr Justice Acton, summed up heavily against Robertson. To the jury he said: 'The evidence of anything even approaching or resembling insanity is so slight that I confess I hesitate as to whether it is not my duty to tell you that there is substantially no such evidence; but I do not propose to take out of your hands the consideration of this question.'

The jury took 25 minutes to return a guilty verdict and the judge passed the death sentence. This jury, unlike the one in the case of Hector Leach in 1926, did not recommend the guilty man to mercy.

An appeal against the verdict and the death sentence was heard at the Court of Criminal Appeal in London on 21 November 1927. Lord Chief Justice Hewart sat on the bench with Mr Justice Avory and Mr Justice Salter. Mr Fyfe said that 'every person, unlike the condemned man, has not had a history of extreme hardship and ill-health and of drinking to such an extent that it preyed on his mind.' However, William Robertson was by no means unique. In the harsh years of the trade depression after the First World War, many men gave up all hope of finding work and turned to crime or drink or to both. Many had taken their own lives.

'There was,' said Fyfe, 'also an observed abnormality immediately after the crime. There was a situation of extreme difficulty and tragedy that even the most balanced mind might be affected by it.'

The Lord Chief Justice, dismissing the appeal, said that the appeal court considered the judge 'would have been entitled to withdraw the whole of the evidence of insanity placed before the jury, as it was so extremely slight.' Mr Fyfe had done all he could. Now only the Home Secretary could save Robertson.

There was no reprieve. William Robertson was hanged at Walton on the morning of 6 December 1927. The executioner was William Pierrepoint, assisted by Thomas Phillips. The drop was 5ft 11in. Death was instantaneous, said the coroner's report. As was usual on these occasions, it was reported that the execution was carried out in 'a skilful, decorous and humane manner'.

Gas

On the evening of Monday 14 November 1927 a 15-year-old girl called Lavinia Cowburn of 42 Belgrave Street in Liscard was found unconscious from gas poisoning in a cabinet-maker's workshop in Park Street, Liscard. At 8.55 p.m. that evening the girl was admitted to the Wallasey Victoria Hospital and died some twenty minutes later from the effects of gas.

The workshop where Lavinia was found was used by 54-year-old George Graham of 88 Seaview Road. Graham was arrested and taken to Manor Road police station where, at 2 a.m., he was charged with murder.

Lavinia Cowburn worked as a telegraphist with the post office in Liverpool. For three weeks or so before her death, Lavinia's work colleagues had noticed that she appeared unwell. After eating her lunch, she used to drink a yellow liquid from a small bottle. The girl's mother had more than once tackled Lavinia about her health and on the morning before she left for her last day at work, Mrs Cowburn had told her daughter that if she didn't improve, she would take her to see a doctor. In fact, as was to be discovered later, Lavinia was eight weeks pregnant.

At 8.30 p.m. on 14 November George Graham turned up at the back door of the Cowburn's house in Belgrave Street and said to Mrs Cowburn: 'I have found Vinnie on the bench,' adding at the same time something about gas. Graham was so agitated that Mrs Cowburn could hardly understand what he was talking about. Following Graham to his workshop in Park Street, Mrs Cowburn found her daughter lying on top of a workbench on the point of death. There was a dreadfully strong smell of gas in the shop.

Mrs Cowburn asked Graham why he had been in his workshop at such a late hour. He replied: 'I came to put the fire out.' Mrs Cowburn went to fetch her son George from a neighbouring concert hall and he carried his sister home. An ambulance was called and the girl was taken to hospital where, to no avail, artificial respiration was tried. She died without regaining consciousness. Lavinia's father was William Cowburn, a telephone engineer, who was then on his way to the Isle of Man on the *Fenella*. A radio message was sent to the ship to call him back home to face the tragedy.

While Mrs Cowburn and George were taking the stricken girl back to Belgrave Street, Graham ran to Manor Road police station and asked for an officer to be sent to Park Street as 'a girl has gassed herself'. He said he did not know the number of the premises, but said: 'It is Mr Graham's furniture workshop.' When asked for his name, Graham started to walk quickly out of the office, saying, 'I am going back there now.'

After making inquiries, Wallasey police arrested Graham at his home, and at 11 p.m. Chief Constable Barry and Inspector Cauldwell went to the workshop with Graham, who was then taken to the police station.

Above the bench on which the girl was found there was a gas bracket from which hung a rubber tube. The other end of the tube was attached to a gas ring wrapped up in sackcloth, on the bench. A bag was also under the sacking, forming a pillow, and a girl's hat was between the sacking and the wall. It was possible that the girl could have rigged up the gas supply and killed herself, but Graham was to say that he and the girl had both agreed to take gas. A suicide agreement would of course mean that Graham, as a surviving member of that agreement, would be liable to a charge of murder.

Later that night, Graham was questioned by Chief Constable Barry, whose replies were taken down in writing. He apparently said: 'I left home at 7.30 p.m. I think I went straight to the workshop to see about the fire, to put it out if it was in. I think I went in with Vinnie Cowburn. I met her a little time before. I believe there was somebody dead. I must be going mad. Who brought me from my workshop?'

Seemingly rambling off the point, Graham continued:

Tell me! I have been down on the railway. I have been seeing the engines tonight. I do not know where I have been since leaving Belgrave Street. I did not know Vinnie Cowburn was dead. I do not remember who undid the door of the workshop. The door was open, I think, when I went in. I don't have the key. I think I have seen that box of pills before. Yes, I bought them and other pills in Liverpool.

After the Chief Constable had cautioned Graham, he made a voluntary statement in which he was alleged to have said:

Yes, I may as well tell you. It has come to me now. We were going to take gas, both of us. We were both on the bench. I remember that now. She was frightened to go home. I have told you the truth. I don't believe in telling lies. I have told you the truth. We both agreed to do it. She drove me to it. In my right senses I would not have dreamed of it. I have been worried in the shop and my wife has been ill. It has preyed on my mind.

On the following day, however, when he was told that he had the right to attend the inquest, Graham said: 'I am not saying what I said last night.'

An inquest was opened by Wallasey Coroner J. C. Bate at 10 a.m. at the Presbyterian Church School in Seacombe. By now, Mr Cowburn had returned from the Isle of Man and he gave formal evidence of the identification of his daughter. Lavinia, he said, was fifteen on 17 March of that year. The inquest was then adjourned until the completion of criminal proceedings against George Graham.

A committal hearing for Graham was held at Wallasey on 6 December 1927. Emma Youd, a 15-year-old probationer telegraphist, said she had known Lavinia Cowburn since the previous April. On the day of the tragedy they walked together along Whitechapel and Church Street in Liverpool where, at about 7.10 p.m., the girl, who had been at her work all day, parted company with Emma when she boarded a tramcar for the Pier Head, on her way back home by ferry to Wallasey.

Another young telegraphist called Harriet Wilkes, 17, said she had noticed a change in Lavinia about three weeks before she died. She was often sick and had been taking a yellow-coloured medicine. The bottle was produced in court.

George Graham had been known to Lavinia Cowburn's parents for some years. He had done small cabinet-making jobs for them. Lavinia had been in the habit of visiting Graham's workshop, a short distance from Belgrave Street. She had made little boxes and other small things for her home. Witnesses were called to prove that Graham and the girl had been on friendly terms for years.

Allan Billington, a French polisher employed by Graham, said he knew the girl and had often seen her at the workshop in Park Street. Graham was not always there when the girl arrived, and when Graham was not there she did not stay. Concerning the key of the workshop, Billington said that the only key he had seen was of a Yale type, with a small piece of wood attached to a string. He then identified the key in court. Sometimes, on closing the workshop, Graham put the key in his pocket; at other times he put it in an outhouse nearby for an upholsterer who came to work in the evening, or for the first-comer in the morning.

Billington described how he left with Graham shortly before 5 p.m. on the fateful day, at which time there had been a good fire burning in the workshop stove. He asked Graham if he should put the fire out and Graham replied, 'No, it's quite all right'. Prosecuting solicitor Saywell was hoping to show that Graham had taken the key with him, thereby disallowing the girl from letting herself into the shop. In reply to Saywell, Billington said that when he and Graham left the shed, Graham did not go to the outhouse where the key was often left. Billington also said he was certain that the key was not left inside the workshop.

Frank Britten, a fruiterer who rented a stable in Park Street, near the workshop, was asked by Mr Saywell about Graham; 'What sort of man did you think him?' Britten replied, 'I should say he was a very dangerous man. If you swore in his presence he would pick you up for it. He was not particular in talking about women. I should call him a religious man in wolf's clothing.'

Witnesses presented evidence which had about it something of the flavour of village gossip. Alfred Mills, a greengrocer who also used a stable in Park Street, said he recalled an occasion one night in the previous January. He said he looked into the shed, which was lit up, saw Graham and the girl there and heard Graham, who was working at the bench, say: 'Listen, there were three girls up here the other day for the greengrocer.'

Laura Hughes, a married woman who lived in Park Street, said she had known Graham for three years. She had often seen Lavinia meeting him in the street. Phyllis Dixon, a young dressmaker from Park Street, said she used to know Lavinia when she was about 13½ or 14 years old and at school. She often saw Graham and the girl together at that time. Alice Hughes, the wife of a coal dealer and also of Park Street, said she had seen Lavinia coming from the workshop at night, up to about 9 p.m. on some occasions.

Liverpool Assizes

In 1823 Liverpool Corporation petitioned the Secretary of State to accord the city the status of an assize town, and on 7 August 1835 the first Liverpool Assizes were held. In 1846 the Corporation bought Newsham House, an eighteenth-century dwelling situated in Newsham Park, for use as a judges' lodging for the circuit udges. One of the notable figures who resided there for the assizes was F. E. Smith, later Lord Birkenhead. In 1971 the assizes were replaced by crown courts, and much of the old pomp and pageantry that usually accompanied the assizes was toned down.

Graham's murder trial at Liverpool Assizes opened on Monday 6 February 1928 and continued into a second day. So great was the public interest that the court was full, and many of those who stood in a long queue outside were unable to gain admission. The judge was Mr Justice Swift, prosecuting counsel were Mr Wingate-Saul KC and Noel Goldie. For the defence were E. G. Hemmerde KC and R. C. Essenhigh. Graham, a man of slender build who wore spectacles, pleaded not guilty in a firm voice.

In his opening presentation of the case against Graham, Mr Wingate-Saul read out the statement which the police said Graham had made in the early hours of the Tuesday morning. However, it soon became clear the Graham may not have been in a fit state to answer questions when he made his incriminating admission. It was also possible that he had not been properly cautioned before some of his remarks.

Sydney Graham, a musician and Graham's son, said that for some time before 14 November his mother's health had been precarious and his father had financial worries. Sydney said he went to look for his father in the workshop late on 14 November, but was unable to find him. On returning home at 11.30 p.m., he found his father sitting in the house, moaning and distressed. Sydney could not get any coherent statement from him and, up to the time of the police taking him away, 'he did not seem to be capable of making a statement, or even of walking'.

A flaw began to appear in the prosecution's case. In cross-examination by Mr Hemmerde, Inspector Cauldwell admitted that when the car carrying Graham arrived at the police station, Graham had to be lifted bodily out of the vehicle. Cauldwell said this was done because 'the car hood was rather low and the step difficult'. According to Cauldwell, Graham was able to walk into the station without help. After the interview at the station, said Cauldwell, Graham, when charged with murder, replied 'Not guilty'.

Chief Constable Barry said that when Graham was brought into the police office he was 'agitated'. In reply to the first few questions, Graham kept repeating 'I don't remember' and 'Oh, how dreadful!' Chief Inspector Ormerod took down his statement. Barry showed Graham a box of pills, which had been found in the workshop's stove, and Graham said he had bought them in Liverpool. He then made a formal statement which was, said Barry, read back to Graham, who then signed it. Commenting on Graham's fitness, Barry said: 'Although agitated, he seemed to be rational, and to appreciate the questions put to him, as well as what he himself was saying.'

Mr Hemmerde, in his cross-examination of Mr Barry, wasted no time.

'Did you ask Dr Martlew whether Graham was in a fit condition to give evidence?'

'No, I did not', Barry replied: 'because he obviously was. He walked into the office without assistance, and sat down.'

After quoting some of the remarks attributed to Graham about 'seeing the engines', and other matters, Mr Hemmerde had more questions for Barry.

'Don't remarks like that indicate that it was rather dangerous to press questions on a man like that?'

'No, because he appeared to me to be evading questions.' And he went on to conclude: 'The questioning I carried out was entirely in accordance with our regulations as laid down by His Majesty's judges.'

On the second day of the trial, Mr Hemmerde called Graham into the witness box to give evidence for his defence. Graham remained calm and self-possessed throughout his own counsel's questions and the cross-examination by Mr Wingate-Saul which followed them.

Graham stated he had lived in Wallasey for twenty years, and that for the past seven months his wife had suffered from 'nervous prostrations'. He also had considerable financial troubles. For the past few years, he said, the girl had been in the habit of visiting his workshop about once a week, but he maintained that there had been 'no familiarity whatever' between them. In October he met the girl on the Liverpool landing stage and they crossed by the ferry together. She spoke to him about herself and he gave her 'certain advice'. As a result of a conversation they had at his workshop on 10 November he again gave her advice. She did not, he said, act on his advice on either occasion. It seems as if the girl had told Graham that she was possibly pregnant and Graham may have been trying to procure a miscarriage.

Describing the events of 14 November, Graham said that in the morning he had put the workshop key in the 'secret place' which was known by his assistant and, he believed, by the girl. That evening he left home with the intention of collecting money for some chairs in Penkett Road, and of then attending to the workshop fire. He decided to see Lavinia Cowburn because he was rather worried about her. He boarded a tramcar and met the girl at Seacombe Ferry at 7.30 p.m.

I gave her advice but no medicine. I left her at the corner of Liscard Road and Martin's Lane, five or six minutes walk from home. I was then very much upset by something her mother was going to do [probably to take her to see a doctor]. I offered to go with her to see her mother, but she would not agree. I set off for Penkett Road but, realising that the journey would be fruitless, because the chairs had not been delivered, I went round to my workshop to see to the fire.

Graham said that when he got there the key was not where he left it and the workshop door was ajar. He went straight to the fire but, hearing groans and smelling gas, he went across to the bench and found the girl lying there. Her face was covered with a sack.

'I turned off the gas, which was hissing out of the tube, took the sack off the girl, shook her and shouted at her.'

He tried to lift the girl off the bench but could not do so. He then went to her mother's house in Belgrave Street.

Mr Wingate-Saul then asked Graham about his time at the police station. Graham said that the last thing he remembered of the events on 14 November was standing by the ambulance and seeing the girl's body being put into it. He said: 'After that I do not remember anything until I was charged with murdering Lavinia Cowburn.'

Defence counsel asked: 'Do you remember being in the Chief Constable's office?'

'No. When I was charged with murder it rather startled me.'

'You have heard the statement which you are alleged to have made?'

'Yes.'

'Have you any recollection whatever of making that statement?'

'None whatever,' said Graham. Graham then said that there was no truth whatever in the suggestion that he and the girl had arranged to die together. He said: 'I had no idea she was contemplating suicide or I would not have left her.'

Questioned about a letter found in the girl's raincoat, Graham said he wrote it about August Bank Holiday. He had promised to give her five shillings if she could do a certain piece of carving with no tool other than her Girl Guide's knife. The girl completed the work successfully and wrote to Graham, asking for the money, when she was away in camp. The letter came to his house. Graham was 'rather upset' because his wife opened it. She wondered why a young girl should be writing to him. He said he thought five shillings was a lot to send at a time, so he wrote to the girl, enclosing two shillings and promising another two the following week.

In cross-examination by Mr Wingate-Saul, Graham said he knew he was doing wrong in providing the girl with medicine. On 14 November

Lavinia told him that her mother was going to take her to a doctor the following day. Graham said: 'She did not seem afraid to go home but she was afraid of seeing the doctor.' He said he had tried to help the girl because she was a friend and seemed to trust him very much. He remembered signing the charge book at the police station, but 'the first I knew about having made a statement was when it was read out in court on 15 November'.

Mr Justice Swift asked Graham: 'How much money did you spend on medicine for the girl?'

'Two pounds four shillings', was the reply.

In his address to the jury, defence counsel Hemmerde said: 'But for the statement made by Graham in the small hours of 15 November, there would be no evidence whatever against him.' Mr Hemmerde contended that Graham should not have been questioned at the police station without being medically examined. He asserted that,

> A statement taken when Graham was labouring under such extreme nervous tension as not to be normal should be regarded as valueless. It would not be safe to act upon admission so obtained. The case put forward by the prosecution that these two people had made a suicide pact is inconsistent with every fact that has been proved in the case.

Little had been heard so far about Lavinia's pregnancy but Mr Justice Swift referred to it when he told the jury,

> After hearing Graham's account of his relationship with the girl during the last three or four weeks of her life, and the fact that he spent £2 4s. of his own money on drugs for a certain purpose, at a time when he could ill afford it, I should think there are few people who cannot imagine that Graham was responsible for her condition. I say that merely to warn you that, if that should be your view, you must take care that it does not assume a disproportionate place in your consideration of this case.

Concerning the validity or otherwise of Graham's statements to the police, the judge said:

> The statement at the police station was taken with perfect propriety and I see no reason to cavil at the way in which the Chief Constable

has acted on the matter. The jury has to make up its mind whether that statement can be realised upon. Except for it, there is no evidence on which the jury can find a suicide pact, and there is no allegation in this case that murder was committed in any other way.

After forty minutes, the jury returned a verdict of 'not guilty'. Graham was discharged and walked out of the dock a free man. A large crowd had gathered outside St George's Hall to await the verdict, but Graham left the building by the north door, practically unobserved.

Two Stabbings

Surveys have shown that one-third of all murders are committed by men against their wives or partners. More often than not, these murders are carried out when the woman has left the man or threatened to leave him. A very dangerous time for the woman is the first three months of separation. After that time the risk of murder is considerably less. The next two cases fall into this category of murder.

At about 11.15 p.m. on Saturday 22 October 1927, a woman was heard screaming and shrieking in Soho Street, off Islington in Liverpool. A few moments later, Mrs Martha Sutherland, 25, who had been living apart from her husband in a lodging house at 87 Soho Street, was found dead in the gutter, with her head almost severed. The husband, George William Sutherland, also 25, a fruit porter lodging in Wilton Street, was arrested and taken to Rose Hill bridewell, where later he was charged with the wilful murder of his wife.

The Sutherlands were married at an Everton church in 1925 but for some time they had been living apart. During this time, Martha had been consorting with various men. George did not take kindly to his wife's way of life and was becoming increasingly angry with her.

On the Saturday night in question, George Sutherland and a man called Shuttleworth were drinking in the Busker's Arms, Islington. Martha was there also, with a man called Rogers. Later that night, after the pubs had shut, at about 10.15 p.m., Sutherland was back in his lodging house. He said to a fellow lodger: 'Where does Joe Rogers live? I would like a few words with him. He was trying to be a bit funny with me on Thursday night.'

At 11 p.m., Sutherland went to look for his wife. He called at her lodging house in Soho Street and, speaking to one of the other lodgers, asked, 'Can I see Maisie?' He was told she was in and then he said: 'You might tell her I want her.'

Martha came out of the house with a plate in her hand and her purse in the other. Then the couple walked together to a chip shop some fifty yards along Soho Street. When Martha emerged from the shop, a quarrel broke out between the couple.

Sutherland drew a razor from his pocket and, dropping her plate of food with a crash onto the pavement, Martha fled down Soho Street, closely pursued by her murderous husband. He grabbed his wife by her bobbed hair and drew the razor's blade across her neck. She fell screaming to the ground. A few seconds later she was dead, drowned in her own blood. Her throat had been cut deeply, almost to the spinal cord.

In the brief struggle, Sutherland had also received an injury, a deep razor cut through his sleeve and into his left arm. As a large crowd of passers-by gathered, Sutherland said to a man named Quinn: 'It's all right, fetch a policeman. I have cut her throat, she is better off.' When Police Constable Jennings arrived on the scene, Sutherland said to him: 'I am your man, officer, I did it with a razor.' He also pointed to a place, a few yards down Mansfield Street, where an open razor lay in the roadway.

At the bridewell, Sutherland was reported to have told Detective Sergeant Pritchard: 'I gave her my razor to set. She had it in her possession. She tried to cut me with it.' Pointing to his left forearm, Sutherland said, 'That's where she got me'. He also said, 'I took it off her and made a belt at her with it'. When charged with murder, Sutherland replied: 'What I did I did to save myself from getting cut.'

George Sutherland came to trial at Manchester Assizes on 22 November 1927. He pleaded not guilty to the charge. It transpired that a witness had seen Mrs Sutherland in conversation with a man, presumably George, outside the chip shop. She was heard to say to him: 'I will go with who I like', and then she assumed a threatening attitude with the plate, lifting it up with her right hand.

The prosecution, led by Mr Laski, alleged that the woman had been leading an immoral life and, Sutherland resenting this, they had separated. On the Saturday night, he berated her for living with another man and then attacked her. The defence, in the hands of Mr Essenhigh, was that earlier in the day Sutherland had given Martha a razor to be adjusted. It was she who first drew the razor and cut George's arm. Sutherland then snatched the weapon with his left hand. Although he was only intending to strike her a backhand blow, he accidentally cut her.

Dr McFall, Professor of Forensic Medicine at Liverpool University, said the woman was pursued, caught probably by her hair and slashed with such force that the weapon jumped from her neck and cut Sutherland on his arm.

There was some evidence that Sutherland had been provoked. A witness called Howey said that she saw Mrs Sutherland strike her husband first. However, this witness was discredited under cross-examination by Mr Laski, who said to the jury, 'If ever there was a broken reed of a witness it must be Bridget Howey'.

In his final address, defence counsel Essenhigh contended that Sutherland was guilty only of manslaughter because he had been provoked by his wife. However, the evidence of provocation was slight.

Sutherland was found guilty of murder and automatically sentenced to death by hanging. After being sentenced, the condemned man said 'Thank you' to the judge.

On 19 December, an appeal was heard at the Court of Criminal Appeal, before a tribunal of the Lord Chief Justice, Mr Justice Avory and Mr Justice Branson. The ground of the appeal was that there was evidence at the trial of 'such provocation as to reduce the crime from murder to manslaughter'. Giving judgement, Lord Hewart said:

> At the trial it was faintly suggested that the crime was committed in self-defence. That is not now relied on. It was suggested that his wife attacked Sutherland with a razor and that he snatched it out of her hand and inflicted the wound which caused her death.

In conclusion, Lord Hewart said:

> There is no evidence of self-defence and no evidence, except the prisoner's and the strange evidence of a woman named Bridget

Howey, of the alleged provocation. It is a perfectly clear case and the appeal is dismissed.

George Sutherland was hanged at Walton on 3 January 1928.

⁂

On the evening of Friday 11 May 1928, 26-year-old Mary Alice Reed, a mill worker of 35 Garibaldi Street, Everton, lay in a critical condition at the Stanley Hospital, suffering from a throat wound. The wound was allegedly inflicted by Alfred George Absalom, an unemployed labourer of Sackville Street, off Roscommon Street. She died in hospital on the following Thursday.

The couple, who had been seeing each other for six years, had begun to get furniture for their future home, but they had recently quarrelled over Alice mixing with other men. On the Friday night they met in Sackville Street. Absalom drew a sailor's knife, struck Alice in the throat, and she fell to the pavement. Absalom was hurrying away when he was stopped by a man who asked him what was the matter. Absalom was said to have replied, 'I have done nothing'. He then threw down a sheath knife and started to run. He was chased by a number of people and initially escaped, but was later arrested by Inspector Platt of the Rose Hill division. The injured woman was taken to hospital where she eventually dictated a deposition in the presence of Absalom in which she said: 'He wanted me to go out with him and I would not. As I was walking away from him he struck the knife into my throat. He did not say anything before he did it.'

Absalom was tried before Mr Justice Talbot and a jury at Liverpool on 15 June 1928. Prosecuting Counsel A. T. Crossthwaite claimed that 'The evidence reveals a deliberate and calculated murder'. He said that on 4 May, a week before the stabbing, Absalom had shown annoyance with Alice because she had been out cycling with a man who had repaired her bicycle. On the afternoon of 11 May, Absalom bought a sheath knife at a cutlery store in St John's Lane. Two hours later, at 6 p.m., said Mr Crossthwaite, he was seen talking to Alice Reed outside St Peter's Church in Sackville Street.

Residents heard the girl's screams and on coming out of their doors, saw her fall to the pavement. The gash in her throat was 1½ inches long and 2½ inches deep. On the way to the police station, Absalom was alleged to have said, 'She won't fool me any more!' At the police station, he continued: 'I did it. I want to be finished with her. She has been playing this game for too long.' The girl's father claimed that there had been a cooling-off on her part but, as far as he knew, she was not friendly with any other man.

Defence counsel Maxwell Fyfe called upon Absalom to give evidence. He said he had no intention to harm the girl. For sometime, said Absalom, he had been managing a fish and chip business for his brother-in-law, and he bought the knife to fillet fish. He said he was taking the knife to the shop when he met Alice Reed in Sackville Street, on her way home.

Describing the stabbing, Absalom told the jury,

> We talked in a friendly way, but I could not get her to say definitely whether she would call to see me at the shop, as she used to. I took out the knife, intending to scare her with a threat to take my own life. She tried to walk away and I put out my right hand to stop her, forgetting that the knife was there. Then I saw blood pouring from her throat.

Absalom continued: 'In a dazed state, I dropped the knife and walked away. The affair was a pure accident. I was so scared at the sight of blood that my mind was a blank as to what happened later.' He said he had no recollection of making the statement to the police or of being present when the girl's deposition was taken.

After forty-five minutes, the jury returned from their room with a request that certain parts of the evidence should be read to them again. This was done. Then R. E. Jackson, house surgeon at the hospital, was recalled to the witness box. In reply to questions by the jury, he said it would in his opinion have required 'considerable force' to inflict the fatal wound. The operation performed on the girl was, he said, 'absolutely necessary'.

'Do you consider she might have lived if she had not been operated upon?', one juror asked.

'No', replied Jackson. 'In my opinion there would have been no possible chance.' He said the wound was not a draw across the neck, but a stab.

After forty more minutes of deliberation the jury returned a guilty verdict, with a strong recommendation to mercy. Addressing Absalom, Mr Justice Talbot said:

You have been found guilty of murder, and upon evidence which made the verdict absolutely inevitable. There is but one sentence which is appointed by the law for that crime, that is the sentence of death, and you must prepare yourself for that. The jury have recommended you to mercy, and that recommendation will be laid before those who have power to give effect to it, but it is my duty to warn you that you are not to count upon my remission of your sentence.

With emotion, the judge pronounced sentence of death. Absalom listened calmly, and the left the dock without assistance.

On Monday 9 July there was an appeal. Mr Fyfe said that the judge was wrong in not leaving the question of manslaughter to the jury. He had dealt wrongly with the wounds on the girl's neck and with the medical evidence. In addition, the judge's direction on the demeanour and action of the accused after the occurrence was wrong.

Dismissing the appeal, however, Lord Hewart said the verdict was correctly described by the judge as inevitable on the evidence before the jury. 'The summing-up is not open to the slightest unfavourable criticism'. Hewart said that the defence raised at the trial was that the wound which killed the woman was inflicted accidentally. Some suggestion was made that the jury might in some way find a verdict of manslaughter, but Hewart said that the judge was quite right in not leaving that alternative to the jury. It was, said Hewart, a clear case. Finally, in his usual blunt manner, Hewart concluded: 'There is nothing in the application and it is dismissed'.

Absalom's execution was fixed for Wednesday 25 July. On the Tuesday the Home Secretary refused to grant a reprieve, so the law had to take its course.

There was a crowd of about two hundred for the 8 a.m. execution at Walton Prison. When the bell tolled eight, men in the crowd doffed their hats and three women wearing black shawls knelt in prayer on the wet pavement. The executioner was Tom Pierrepoint of Bradford, assisted by Henry Pollard of Blackburn. City Coroner Mort carried out an inquest. The verdict was 'Death by judicial hanging, carried out in accordance with the law'.

The Pierrepoint family

In this book and in *Murder in Edwardian Merseyside*, the reader may have noticed that quite a number of executions were performed by members of the Pierrepoint family. Three members of this family became, in turn, the Official Executioner of Great Britain and Ireland. Between the three of them they took part in approximately 800 executions, a sobering figure.

Henry Pierrepoint (1874–1922) badgered the Home Office to become a hangman, taking up the job after a period of training in 1901; he wanted to travel and this job would enable him to do so. He in turn encouraged his brother Thomas (1870–1954) to follow him in this line of work. Henry had given Thomas some training in a disused stables in the yard behind his home which contributed to his successful application.

Finally, Henry's son Albert (1905–1992) took up this profession, acting as assistant to his uncle and later becoming Official Executioner in 1940. Henry and Thomas hanged murderers, but Albert would also hang spies, traitors and Nazis after the judgements of the Nuremburg trials. Among the war criminals he dispatched was Josef Kramer, the 'Beast of Belsen', and Irma Grese, a very young (22) and notorious concentration camp guard. Albert would be the most prolific of the three, hanging around 400 people, including individuals whose names and cases are still recognised today: Ruth Ellis, Derek Bentley, John Christie and William Joyce, also known as 'Lord Haw Haw'.

The Pierrepoints kept meticulous records of all the executions they did, including height, weight, length of drop, and time and place of execution. Henry made a note of the state of the prisoner's neck, but when Albert wrote his records he did not include this detail as he felt it distasteful. Albert retired in 1956 and later published an autobiography entitled *Pierrepoint – Executioner* in 1974. Despite his prolific record as a hangman Albert Pierrepoint did not defend or uphold the death penalty, as a couple of quotes from him illustrate:

It did not deter them then and it had not deterred them when they committed what they were convicted for. All the men and women I have faced at that final moment convince me that in what I have done I have not prevented a single murder ... I have come to the conclusion that executions solve nothing, and are only an antiquated relic of a primitive desire for revenge which takes the easy way and hands over the responsibility for revenge to other people.

Teddy Bear

On the morning of Sunday 28 October 1928, church-going pedestrians in Northbrook Street, Princes Park, were startled by a young woman rushing out of the house at 110, half-dressed and bleeding from throat wounds, screaming 'Save me! Save me!' She was 19-year-old Mary Agnes Fontaine, who lived with her mother Mrs Alice Fontaine, a widow aged 47. The household was completed by a young man called Joseph Clarke, 21, who lodged with the two women as a boarder. Inside the house, Mrs Fontaine was found strangled. Standing at the house door was Clarke, who asked a passer-by to get a policeman. When one came he was arrested and next day Clarke appeared at the police court before the stipendiary magistrate, Stuart Deacon. The charges were the murder of Alice Fontaine and the attempted murder of her daughter Mary, who was known affectionately as May.

Inquiries into Joseph Clarke's background revealed that he was a well educated young man. At the age of 16, he visited his mother in the United States, where he had studied at Princeton University. While in the States he took lessons in psychology and hypnotism, and on returning to England, Clarke made it known that he was a hypnotist and embarked upon a campaign of the seduction of women on a large scale. Several women who had known Clarke declared that he had a magnetic personality. Letters and poems which he wrote illustrated his considerable literary ability and his drawings showed great talent.

Clarke met May Fontaine in May 1928. Subsequently he lodged in her mother's house in Northbrook Street, calling himself Reginald Kennedy. During his five-month stay there, the friendship between Clarke and May ripened into one of mutual affection. The couple used endearing names for each other. He called her 'Bouffe' and she called him 'Teddy Bear'.

As time passed, Clarke would not pay his keep to Mrs Fontaine, until eventually she let him stay in the house without any payment at all. His presence in the household became tedious for Mrs Fontaine but, because of May's affection for the young man, she took no action. Mr Digby Seymour, prosecuting solicitor in the police court, described Clarke as 'nothing more or less than a parasite, bartering on the kindness of two defenceless women'. They were, said Seymour, frightened of Clarke, and as events turned out the women's fears were well justified.

Joseph Clarke did not try to deny killing Mrs Fontaine and attacking her daughter. In fact, he dictated a long, detailed confession to the crimes. Mr Seymour read out the confession in court, and very chilling reading it made:

> I am 21 years of age, of no fixed occupation. I have been going to sea as a pantryman. Since April last I have been carrying on a little business as a wireless engineer.

After being cautioned, he continued:

> I know what that means. An hour ago I had no more intention of murdering anyone than I had of flying. I do not know what happened, but Mrs Fontaine was talking to me about getting on, making good. She was just saying that I could get a job and make a home for May, her daughter.

> I can't tell you what happened then, but I suddenly put my hands on her throat, and I threw her over the arm of the chair. She screamed 'Oh, Teddy Bear!' (that was the name she used to call me). I just pressed her throat good and hard for about a minute. She stopped breathing. We were in the room alone at the time. She had just brought me a cup of tea.

> I had been wandering about all night. I came to the house about 9.30. I had been lodging with Mrs Fontaine since about June lst last.

Mrs Fontaine and I had grown unfriendly, because I could not pay my way. She was always very good to me all the time. She lent me money and tried her best to help me to get along.

When Mrs Fontaine had finished gasping I went to the bedroom of Miss Fontaine and I asked her if she still loved me. She replied: 'You know I always will'. I said to her: 'I have killed mother, and because you have turned me down, I am going to kill you too'. I gripped her by the throat, but she screamed and struggled fiercely.

We disarranged all the furniture in the room, but I eventually got her under control. Her lips turned black, but all of a sudden she revived, and struggled more fiercely than ever. I thought her screams would have attracted the whole street. There are some pieces of electric light cord upstairs, one of which I tied around her throat. She began to gasp like her mother. Then I suddenly realised I was killing her. I had in my pocket a shoemaker's knife and I cut the cord with that, and tried to bring her to.

She screamed afresh, then I cut her throat. She seemed to go under for a time, and then she recovered and took me by the hand. She said: 'Let us sit on the bed for a bit, Teddy Bear. You know I loved you. Why have you done all this?' I said: 'I thought you meant to give me up', and she replied: 'How could you think that? I love you still. Let us go and see mother' – still holding me by the hand.

I said: 'For God's sake don't go'. She said: 'You must, Teddy Bear, and tell her you are sorry'. She let go of my hand and went downstairs. I called to her: 'In there, dear, in the sitting room'. She replied: 'Oh no, she is down here'. I was followed downstairs. She went towards the living room on the ground floor. Then she ran out into the street before I could detain her. I went out on the doorstep. She had vanished, but I could hear her screaming. I asked a man standing by to call a policeman. I stood in the doorway until one came.

A committal hearing for Clarke started on 5 November and continued on the 21st and 22nd of the month. Mr Seymour, prosecuting, said that on the morning of the tragedy, Mrs Fontaine opened her cellar door and Clarke came out. She took him to the sitting room as he said he wished to speak privately to her. Mr Seymour continued:

We know what happened in that room, for almost immediately after his arrest Clarke calmly and deliberately confessed how he threw the deceased over the arm of a chair – in which position she would be helpless – and slowly strangled her. He had then gone in to the girl's bedroom to take her life but, by the mercy of Providence, the girl escaped. She had struggled for her life and the condition of the room almost beggars description.

May Fontaine, now recovered from her attack of eight days earlier, in low distinct tones, told the story of her ordeal with Clarke in the bedroom. He had come to her door, and putting both hands on her shoulders, said: 'You know how much I love you. That is why I am going to do this'. He seized her by the throat, and when she called for help, he said: 'You need not call for your mother. I have killed her'. He banged her head on the floor, and the next thing she remembered was that he had cut her throat.

While Clarke was in Wales he sent May a telegram. He made it look like it came from a doctor. Sent from Llanrug, near Caernarfon, it read: 'Young man, Kennedy, delirious condition. Critical. Come immediately. Death may result if you do not. Wire train to cottage, waiting, urgent – Scott, physician.'

During Clarke's stay in Wales he told May to open and forward any letter that came for him. One letter, said May, was from a young lady in Nova Scotia who, it seemed, expected to marry Clarke.

Because Clarke had dispensed with the services of a solicitor, he was entitled to cross examine the prosecution witnesses at the committal. Clarke said he wished to question Miss Fontaine. In steady precise tones he put his questions, referring from time to time to his pencilled notes. Clarke asked: 'Did I not tell you I had given up this girl and was no longer interested in her?' 'Yes', replied May. She then admitted that it had occurred to her that the sudden removal of her affection would unbalance Clarke's mind.

When the hearing was resumed on 21 November, Mr Seymour announced that fresh and important evidence had come into his possession. He recalled Miss Fontaine to the witness box and at one point in May's evidence, Clarke protested excitedly. After a word from magistrate Joseph Lucas, Clarke apologised and sat down again. Clarke was a man of slight build and clean-cut features with his long dark hair brushed back. There was the scab of a cut on his forehead. Throughout the proceedings, he remained remarkably composed.

May Fontaine said that when Clarke returned from Wales he complained that the letters he sent to her had been returned, and he asked her: 'Are you going to give me up?' May explained that her mother sent her to Ireland to be out of his way. Clarke told her, 'If you do give me up I will kill you'. She said she was not frightened by his threat. As she left him he handed her a cobbler's knife, saying 'Take this for me'. She had taken the knife home and put it in a drawer. Later, when she searched for it she could not find it.

On 22 October, six days before the attacks, May again saw Clarke. In the course of their conversation he threatened to 'do her in' if she gave him up. She told him that if he 'did not do something' she had made arrangements to go into a convent for a while, out of his way. Clarke had then told her 'That was all your mother's idea'.

Before questioning May Fontaine, Clarke declared:

I would like to say that last week I dispensed with the services of my solicitor. Communications have been sent to my parents in America, and until I receive funds from them I will represent myself. I understand I will be given full facilities.

Then, speaking to May, he asked: 'You said I would do you in. Did you really believe I would do you in?' May replied 'I believe you said it to frighten me more than anything else'.

'Did you really intend to give me up?'

'No'. May then said that she had never heard him threaten to kill her mother.

On the third and last day of the committal hearing, a detective called Harry Tomlin came into the story. He had been called in by Mrs Fontaine and had warned Clarke to keep away from her daughter. In evidence, Tomlin said that on 18 October, in Clarke's presence, Mrs Fontaine repeated a complaint against Clarke in which she said 'I have been like a mother to him, but he is the biggest liar I have ever met, and the greatest hand at making promises which he never fulfils'. She was afraid, she said, to have him about the place.

Tomlin said he warned Clarke to keep away from the Fontaines, to which Clarke replied, 'Well it is darned hard lines. That is the first real home I have ever had. I know you think I ought to be flogged, and perhaps it would do me good'.

When Clarke cross examined Tomlin, his composure began to desert him and he became excited in his speech. Under a rapid fire of questions, Tomlin admitted that he had advised the girl to give Clarke up.

'I told Miss Fontaine in the presence of her mother that I knew a lot about this man. He has been in prison for fraud.'

'Did you suggest to Miss Fontaine that if she married me I would turn her out on to the streets to sell herself to other men?', Clarke asked Tomlin.

'No', said Tomlin, 'I didn't put it that way. I told her that as far as she was concerned, you were an unknown man and anything might happen. I told her that to my knowledge many girls had ended in a life of shame through associating with unknown men.'

'You meant to imply that you thought I was quite capable of putting a girl on the streets?', Clarke replied.

'I said I thought you were capable of anything.'

Clarke then announced that he wished to make a statement on oath. This statement supplemented his earlier confession in an apparent attempt to show himself in a better light. Clarke seemed to be enjoying the attention he received in court. Picking up a sheaf of papers, he started to read, in precise and distinct tones, another sickening version of the murder of Mrs Fontaine:

> I wish to make it known that in the statement I made to the detective inspector, on the occasion of my apprehension on the charge of murder and attempted murder, that I deliberately suppressed certain details in the tragedy which I know wish to make known. I am perfectly aware of the magnitude and importance of this statement, and I believe I am in such mental condition as to form a clear judgement on the matter, and find the following assertions satisfactory to my conscience at the time. My statement on the aforementioned date is completely true, except for the following:

> After I had pressed Mrs Fontaine's throat for the space of a minute, maintaining a very considerable pressure for that period, I relaxed my grip and the deceased lady recovered sufficiently, for approximately a minute and a half, to murmur some words which were

just audible. I had then recovered my mental balance sufficiently to realise what I had done, and in a sincere endeavour to help her to recover, I put my arms round her chest and tried my utmost to raise her and place her in the chair. Unfortunately, I had not sufficient strength. I supported her weight, taking it off her neck as best I could, and knelt beside her.

In my arms she murmured ordinarily, 'Teddy Bear, I am dying', which was followed by two messages to be given to her daughter May and to Sonny, her son in South Africa. I do not think it necessary to disclose these messages in court. The messages, which were very short, were immediately followed by the words 'Goodbye, Teddy Bear. You must always take care of your Bouffe'. The deceased lady smiled on me, who was the cause of her death.

Immediately after that, the sole thought occupying my mind was that I was done for, that I would never have 'Bouffe' and that rather than have her fall into the clutches of that hell-fiend detective (Tomlin), I would kill her. This line of thought caused a kind of frenzy to develop in my mind, although I can distinctly remember I was outwardly calm. My hands were steady and my movements deliberate. I crept downstairs, got the knife from the drawer in the sideboard, slipped it into my coat pocket, and crept back into the sitting room. Mrs Fontaine was quite dead then, and I immediately left the room, closing the door behind me, which sound it was that Miss Fontaine heard before my appearing before her.

The last part of Clarke's statement was as hideous as it was ridiculous.

I have given complete details of what happened in her bedroom, excepting that when Miss Fontaine was unconscious on the floor, when I was trying to bring her to, I showered kisses on her poor discoloured face, and whispered to her that I had tried to kill her only to save her from that awful fellow. I would like to congratulate Miss Fontaine in her presence of mind in eventually getting away from me. But she was quite safe then, as I was again in a normal state of mind, but strengthless.

The trial of Joseph Reginald Victor Clarke for the murder of Alice

Fontaine, held at Liverpool on 4 February 1929, was one of the shortest ever murder trials. It lasted a mere 4½ minutes.

This was mainly due to the prisoner's plea of guilty to a charge of murder carrying the death penalty. Throughout the whole procedure, Clarke seemed totally unmoved. His attentive expression never changed as he answered Mr Justice Finlay's questions firmly. After the indictment had been read out, Clarke, a native of Hilgay in Norfolk, was called upon to plead. He replied in a steady voice: 'I plead guilty'.

Mr Justice Finlay said to Clarke: 'You thoroughly understand that you are pleading guilty to a charge of wilful murder, and thoroughly understand what the only sentence can be which follows that?'

'Yes, my lord', replied Clarke.

'You have thoroughly and clearly thought it over and understand?'

'Yes, my lord'.

'Very well', replied the judge.

In reply to the clerk of assize, Clarke said he had nothing to say. The judge then passed sentence of death in the usual form. The only sign of emotion Clarke gave was a nervous twitching of his fingers when the judge came to the words 'hanged by the neck until you are dead'. 'Thank you, my lord' were Clarke's words after sentence had been passed.

An appeal, submitted in writing by Clarke, was heard at the Court of Criminal Appeal before Justices Avory, Horridge and Rowlatt. Avory read out Clarke's statement:

> I pleaded guilty to a charge of murder which I had not actually committed, and which I had no cause or reason to commit. In offering a plea of guilty I knew full well the consequences, and I beg to bring to your notice the true reasons why I did so. The reasons are that because I felt that since it appeared that I was the direct cause of death to someone who had been most kind to me, I must take the full consequences, because I knew very well it would put a heavy strain and severe ordeal to a witness who was in a very delicate state of health, and whom I wished to save from any further pain and embarrassment.

Clarke also said: 'Counsel for my defence proposed the necessity of offering a plea of temporary insanity as my defence. This I could not possibly countenance'. However, Clarke did say that the attacks were not premeditated. He also pointed out that the post mortem examination found that the dead woman's lungs were unhealthy, and that possibly she would not have died if she had been a thoroughly healthy and sound woman.

Concerning Clarke's attack on Miss Fontaine, Avory said: 'It was only by heroic struggles that this woman escaped from him and managed to make her way downstairs. The appellant omits all reference to what took place after he left the mother for dead.'

Finally, Mr Justice Avory said:

> The Court can only come to the conclusion that defence counsel rightly advised Clarke that the only possible defence to the charge would be a plea of temporary insanity, but the Court is also driven to the conclusion that Clarke himself was right when he said that no such plea could have been successful. There is nothing to justify the Court in interfering with Clarke's confession and the conviction recorded on it. The application, therefore, is dismissed.

Miss Fontaine paid frequent visits to Clarke in the condemned cell. On the morning of the execution, Tuesday 12 March, May attended mass at St Bernard's Church in Kingsley Road. She had sent a personal letter to King George V, appealing for Clarke's life to be spared, but there would be no mercy for the murderer of Alice Fontaine.

At two minutes before the fatal hour of 8 a.m., May was joined in the church by a woman friend who had given her shelter during Clarke's trial and imprisonment. Pierrepoint and Pollard made the necessary arrangements for the hanging of Clarke. Father Lane, who had attended Clarke in the condemned cell, was present at the execution.

It was not until 8.30 a.m. that the two women left and made their way home. Miss Fontaine was dressed in deepest mourning.

Her Secret Life

At about 1 p.m. on Wednesday 13 March 1929, Annie Stewart, a 31-year-old mother of two little boys, dashed wildly out of her house at 11 Prince's View, off Hesketh Street, and into a shop on Lark Lane. Her face and arms were smeared red with blood. Mrs Gallagher, the shopkeeper, was serving a customer called Mrs Bennett. The demented woman, in a voice of frenzy, cried out: 'I have murdered my two children!'

Incredulously, Mrs Gallagher asked the woman what she meant, as if she could not understand what she saw. Mrs Stewart, waving her arms excitedly, cried 'Come with me!' The two women followed Mrs Stewart to her house. In the front parlour of the single-storey cottage were two little boys with their throats cut. They were lying in pools of blood, with which the walls and the furniture were spattered. A bloodstained razor lay close to the children.

The boys were Norman Moffat Stewart, age 7, and 5-year-old Gordon Frederick Stewart. The elder boy was presumed to be dead when the neighbours entered the house, but the younger one lived for a few minutes. The boys were taken by ambulance to the Royal Children's Infirmary in Myrtle Street, where both were pronounced to be dead.

Meanwhile, a message had been sent to Lark Lane police station and detective officers and uniformed men arrived within a few minutes. Mrs Stewart, in a highly hysterical condition, was placed under arrest. Initially, she was allowed to sit in a neighbour's house and then, at about 3 p.m., weeping bitterly, she was taken away in a police van.

Annie Stewart had been deeply attached to her two sons. Twice daily she used to meet them from their school in St Michael's Hamlet and bring them home across the busy Aigburth Road. Neighbours described Mrs Stewart as a steady woman and an affectionate mother. She and the children often went out to meet her husband Norman in the evenings on his way home from the warehouse in town where he worked as a packer. Annie had lived at 11 Prince's View for most of her life. Her parents had lived there before her marriage.

On the morning after the killings, Annie Stewart appeared at the Dale

Street Police Court and was remanded in custody. Sobbing convulsively, she was half-carried from her cell into the dock by two wardresses and a constable. She presented a pathetic figure as she pressed her tear-stained face against the arm of the wardress who supported her.

Police inquiries had unearthed details of Annie Stewart's secret private life, and as a result a man called Henry Senar, a 34-year-old ship's steward of 192 Upper Mann Street, was charged with no fewer than three charges connected with the killings. As well as being charged with the murder of the two boys and of aiding and abetting Annie Stewart to kill them, Senar was additionally charged with 'counselling, procuring and commanding' Mrs Stewart to murder her sons. Senar appeared at the police court before two magistrates – Colonel Wilson and Mr J. Lucas.

Eight months earlier, unknown to Norman Stewart, his wife had become acquainted with Henry Senar after a chance meeting in Sefton Park. Later, they used to meet in the park and elsewhere. Mr Digby Seymour elaborated:

> He has, moreover, been to her home. In fact, on the morning of the murder of the children, at 10 a.m., a man walked through the back door of the house without knocking and went inside. The witness who saw the man going into the house has identified him as Senar.

There was more. Seymour continued:

> At 12.30 that morning, Mrs Stewart appeared to be nervous about the man having been to her house, and she enquired from her neighbours if he had been seen to enter. The murder was committed at 1 p.m. and at 12.45 a boy will say he saw one of the children go to the man and speak to him, telling him that his mother wanted him to go into the house again. The man and the child returned to the house. That boy has identified Senar as being the man.

Chief Inspector Burgess, giving evidence of arrest, said: 'Last night I sent for Senar and saw him in my office. After Senar had made a statement I told him I was not satisfied with his explanation and was going to detain him.' Burgess said he saw Senar later at the main bridewell and read three charges over to him, in reply to which Senar said 'Not guilty'. At the close of the hearing Senar was remanded in custody to await the committal proceedings two days later. As he left the dock Senar exclaimed: 'The charges are ridiculous!'

Senar was a married man with four children, the eldest of whom was eight years old. He had been out of work since Christmas. Before that, he had served as a steward on the Canadian Pacific Line. He had just signed on the liner *Montrose* and should have sailed on 4 April. Senar and his family had lived in an apartment in Upper Mann Street for about two years and neighbours spoke of him as a quiet man who was very fond of his children.

On 5 April a two-day committal hearing for Senar opened at the police court (Annie Stewart had already been committed for trial). An undelivered letter, said to have been written by Mrs Stewart to Senar, was read out. Among those in court were the two spouses, Mrs Senar and Mr Stewart. On leaving at the luncheon adjournment, Mrs Senar fainted, and a witness, Mrs Louisa Thomas, who had charge of Mrs Senar's baby, also collapsed. Senar, who was not legally represented, followed the proceedings closely. He cross examined one of the witnesses at some length about his alleged visits to Mrs Stewart's home. There was drama when, on receiving one reply, Senar exclaimed: 'You did not say that before! You ought to give a man a fair go. I am fighting for my life!'

Suggesting a motive for the crimes, Mr Seymour said:

It had already been disclosed that Annie Stewart declared that she murdered her children. She indicated that she lost her nerve and could not commit suicide. It may be that there was between the accused and Mrs Stewart some pact to rid themselves of their lives and to take with them those two innocent children. It may also be that these two children knew too much of the liason between their mother and Senar. In their innocence, in view of the fact that the father knew nothing of the relationship between the mother and Senar, they might possibly at some time or other have disclosed the fact that a man had called at the house.

Another letter, headed 'Mrs O'Brien, 11 Prince's View', was also produced in court. Norman Stewart identified the writing as that of his wife, who had never mentioned Senar's name to him, nor had he ever seen Senar before. Mrs O'Brien was Annie Stewart's sister. She denied that the letter was in her handwriting, saying that it was in her sister's hand. Mary

O'Brien said she had never written to a man named Harry, nor had she given her sister permission to use her name in the letter. She did not know Senar and had never heard her sister speak of him. The letter was read out to Mr Seymour:

My Dear Harry,

Well love, I am sending you this little parcel. I have been waiting all this time for a letter from you, and not yet had one. I think it is mean of you after promising. I have sent six letters to you, but never had a reply from one. I think it is too bad of you. If you do not want to see me any more will you let me know? That is, if you can find it in your heart to do so. Well love, I don't want to offend you, but it has hurt me so much I cannot help it, not hearing from you all this time. Heaps of love and kisses, your ever loving little girl, Annie.

Following the signature were a number of crosses.

Arthur Thair, chief steward on the steamship *John Holt*, on which Senar served one voyage as second steward, said: 'When Senar was paid off on 27 December last, he asked me not to send any letters or parcels which came addressed to him, but to keep them until he collected them.' On 25 January, Thair's vessel left Liverpool for West Africa, and on the homeward voyage a parcel addressed to Senar was received at Las Palmas. This was taken charge of by the police at Liverpool. As well as the letter, the parcel contained three ties and three pairs of socks.

Senar had allegedly been seen going into the Stewart house on two separate occasions on the morning of the killings. Mrs Louisa Thomas of Siddeley Street said she and Annie had met Senar and another man in Sefton Park 'about nine months ago'. She said that on three subsequent occasions, when calling on Annie, she saw Senar at the house. Once, she said, she saw Annie writing a letter to Senar while he was at sea.

Mrs Christina Calland of 14 Aigburth View, whose back door was opposite that of the Stewarts, said that at about 10 a.m. on the morning of 13 March, she saw a man go into 11 Prince's View by the back door without knocking. She had identified him as Senar in a line-up with seven other men at the Essex Street bridewell.

Little nine-year-old Arthur Banks of 13 Prince's View said he was sent on an errand at 12.45 p.m. on 13 March. Going along the entry at the back of his home, Arthur saw the two Stewart boys approach a man standing by the back door. The boy was near enough to hear Norman say 'My mother wants you'. The man made no reply, but went with the two brothers into their house by the back door. The boy Banks pointed out Senar in court as being the man.

The second day of the committal was devoted to evidence from the police. Detective Constable Bowyer told the court that Senar, while at Essex Street bridewell on 2 April, said he had intended seeing the police, but 'his heart failed him'. He had also thought of committing suicide. Detective Sergeant Appleyard said that when Senar was searched, the police found on him a newspaper cutting containing a photograph of Mrs Stewart and the two boys.

A statement, said to have been made to Detective Chief Inspector Burgess, was then read. In this statement, Senar admitted making the acquaintance of Annie Stewart in Sefton Park and seeing her in the park 'on about four occasions'. He denied having met her anywhere else. The last time he saw her was a week or ten days before the tragedy:

> I never have been in her house in my life. I was not there on the day of the murder. I was alone in the park from 2 p.m. to 5 p.m. I signed for the dole between 9.30 and 10 a.m. and then went to the North Docks. I saw a number of stewards there. I cannot mention any names for that particular day.

Burgess said that when Senar was asked if he objected to being put up for identification, he replied: 'No, I am quite willing. I was not there and never have been there'. Later, when told he would be detained, Senar said: 'Don't let my wife know the charge.' On being charged, his reply was 'I am not guilty'. When told that the City Analyst had discovered human bloodstains on his clothing, Senar said nothing.

At the end on the hearing, before being committed for trial, Senar was asked if he had anything to say. He replied: 'I knew nothing about it, sir. I know nothing about the crime.' He was granted legal aid.

On Monday 15 April 1929 at St George's Hall, before Mr Justice Shearman and a jury, Henry Senar and Annie Stewart were tried together for the murder of Mrs Stewart's two little boys. Both pleaded not guilty. Senar was defended by Maxwell Fyfe, Mrs Stewart by Basil Neild. Sir Reginald Mitchell Banks KC led the prosecution.

Outlining the prosecution case, Sir Reginald said that 'to all outward appearances, Mrs Stewart and her husband were happy, but Mrs Stewart for some time had had a secret life'. On the morning of the tragedy, Mrs Stewart borrowed a razor from a nearby hairdresser.

> The evidence shows that the woman had meditated doing the deed for some hours, and the inference should be drawn – unless Senar can give some satisfactory explanation of his presence so soon before the crime and of the bloodstains – that he shared in the murder.

Husband Norman Stewart said that his married life had been 'pretty good'. He denied that he had ever struck his wife, and also said that since the death of her mother twelve months before, she had been depressed. In cross-examination by Basil Neild, Mr Stewart said that he did not know that his wife, when a girl of about sixteen, had attempted to commit suicide. On the Monday before the crime, he and Annie went to the pictures and saw a film called *The Wind*, a heavy melodrama.

'Was there a murder in it?' asked Neild.

'No', replied Stewart. 'A woman lost her senses in the picture through the wind and rain beating against a window. Afterwards, my wife said the picture had got on her nerves.'

Chief Inspector Burgess read a statement from Mrs Stewart in which she described the murders in a ghastly confession:

> He used to knock me about while mother was alive. He would not let me have any company in the house, not even a young girl . . . I felt unhappy this morning that I thought of doing myself in. At five minutes to one I called Norman into the parlour and first killed one and then I killed the other. I called Gordon. He ran out and cried and I called him back again and he came in. I then cut his throat. When I saw the blood I could not kill myself. I made three attempts to kill the children, but I could not do it. I do not remember doing it. I cut their throats with a razor.

Examining the stained clothing, the judge said: 'If he put a bloody hand in his pocket there would be a great deal more stain than that.' There was a murmur of excitement in court when, at the close of the evidence for the prosecution, Mr Justice Shearman expressed his opinion that there was insufficient evidence to safely convict Senar of murder. 'Nobody saw him running away from the house, and when the woman made a statement she did not mention his name. Anybody holding those children would have been soaked in blood.' He added:

> I have no criticism to offer of the case having been brought. If Senar had been candid in his answers to the police there probably would have been an end to the matter, but I do not think there is sufficient evidence on which a jury can convict him.

Because at the trial stage Senar was charged with murder, he could not be convicted of anything else. The jury, after a brief consultation, found Senar not guilty and he was released.

On behalf of Mrs Stewart, Basil Nield submitted a defence of insanity and called medical evidence to support his claim.

Dr Horace Cole of Mill Street said he attended Mrs Stewart when she was sixteen for attempted suicide. He said her mother's death was 'attended by mental disorder'. He had found signs of mental derangement in two of her sisters.

Professor McFall of Liverpool University said that he believed the woman was insane when she committed the crime:

> The bloodstained knife she saw at the pictures may have suggested a means by which she could commit suicide. She went into the room where the boys were and saw red, which is not mere phraseology, but a definite condition of the mind, and committed the deed.

Dr Robert Walmsley said that Mrs Stewart was suffering from depressive insanity and would not know she was killing her children.

Two prison doctors were then called by the prosecution. Dr Ahern of Walton said that he had made a prolonged examination of the accused, and had been unable to discover any sign of mental disease in her. Dr Watson of Brixton said that from both the legal and the medical points of view, Mrs Stewart knew what she was doing at the time of the crime.

In his summing up, the judge said that perhaps Senar and Mrs Stewart had decided to have nothing more to do with each other and this had affected her mind. The judge said to the jury:

> To my mind the profound common sense of our law is that it is left to the jury to say whether a person is sane or insane. Although you may pay great attention to the experts, it is for you to be satisfied. There is undoubtedly a taint in the family.

After ten minutes' absence, the jury returned to court with a verdict: 'Guilty, but insane at the time'. Before Mrs Stewart was taken away to a secure hospital, permission was given for her husband Norman to see her and to say his farewells.

Mojo

On Thursday 11 July 1929, William Thompson, a 48-year-old labourer, was arrested and charged with committing grievous bodily harm to his wife Ellen Thompson, 45, at their home in Gerard Street.

The alleged crime stemmed from a domestic argument involving, on Mrs Thompson's part at least, a large quantity of alcohol. What made the incident even more serious was that, on the following Sunday morning, Mrs Thompson passed away in Mill Road Infirmary. As an immediate result of her death, William Thompson was charged with wilful murder.

It seems that there was some kind of quarrel in the house and Thompson was seen leaving with a bandage held to his eye, which was trickling blood. Later, his wife was found on the doorstep in a seriously injured condition. She said her injuries had been inflicted by her husband. On the Sunday afternoon, Detective Sergeant Albert Smith went into Walton Prison and told Thompson that his wife had died, and formally cautioned him and charged him. Thompson stated: 'I am not guilty of the murder'.

Thompson made four brief appearances at the police court while preparation was made for the committal proceedings. These then opened on Tuesday 6 August 1929. Acting for Thompson was solicitor Sydney Silverman, who was later to become MP and a staunch opponent of capital punishment. Mr Bishop was the prosecuting solicitor.

Mr Silverman took the unusual course of objecting to the depositions taken in hospital from Mrs Thompson being admitted as evidence against his client. After evidence from neighbours had been heard, Mr Silverman submitted that the depositions, taken at Mill Road Infirmary in the presence of Thompson, were not admissible as evidence. He argued that Thompson had not had a full opportunity to cross examine his wife on her statement. This was because Thompson was warned that the depositions were to be taken only very shortly after his arrest, and before he was actually charged with any offence.

Mr Silverman read out most of the statement allegedly made by Mrs Thompson at the infirmary. It read:

> My husband quarrelled with me. Then he gave me a belt in the face with his hand, and when he got me down he kicked me on the face and stamped me in the guts and all over the body. He was wearing big boots at the time. When I saw he was going too far, I picked up a knife and hit him with it to protect myself. I got downstairs as best I could and then the neighbours came. I remember nothing more.

In answer to questions put to her by her husband, Mrs Thompson said: 'I am sure you stamped on me. I did not fall downstairs. I walked down.'

Mr Silverman suggested that the statement 'cried out for cross-examination', and yet the accused man 'had not had any opportunity of preparing for what was probably the most difficult task in the world, even for a skilled advocate, the task of questioning a woman lying seriously ill'.

Magistrate F. J. Richardson disagreed with Mr Silverman. He ruled that the depositions were admissible, whereupon Silverman submitted that in spite of that ruling, there was still no case to answer. He said: 'There is not a shred of evidence that Thompson ever quarrelled with his wife, or that he had ever struck her, or if he was ever anything but on the best of terms with her.' A woman called Mrs Flynn said she had heard Thompson admitting he had kicked his wife, but this was negatived by a man called Goldbourne who was present when the admission was alleged to have been made.

After a brief adjournment, the magistrate ruled that there was a case to answer. When Mr Silverman applied for a short adjournment to consider the advisability of putting Thompson in the witness box, and the proceedings were adjourned for the day.

Next morning, Thompson occupied the witness box for four hours.

This was unusual at the committal stage. A defence was generally reserved for the trial proper.

Thompson said that when he came home on the afternoon of 10 July, he found his wife with two other women. They were drinking. Referring to methylated spirits, Thompson said to them, 'Hello, what's the game here, more Mojo?' Later, said Thompson, he returned to the house and found that his wife was having 'a seizure'. When she recovered he tried to persuade her to go to bed, but she refused. After the two women had gone, his wife started singing. He remonstrated and after a few words, she said: 'If you are not blind, I will blind you!' and struck him in the eye with a bread knife.

Thompson testified: 'She made another blow at me, but I caught her by both arms, made her drop the knife, and then flung her away from me towards the table. I never had her on the floor at all and never struck her. I went out immediately after that to get my eye attended to.'

Thompson said he met a neighbour called Robert Goldbourne and had a drink with him before reaching the Northern Hospital. Thompson denied talking to Mrs Flynn in the public house. As far as he knew, at that time his wife was all right. He spent the rest of the evening with Goldbourne and did not hear that his wife had been taken to hospital until much later. Cross examined by Mr Bishop, Thompson maintained that he had never touched his wife after throwing her against the table. He heard from someone that his wife had fallen downstairs.

Robert Goldbourne, a carter living at 25 Gerard Street, and Thompson's companion on 10 July, said he had known William and his wife for about thirty years, but had been close friends of theirs for two years. Describing the events of 10 July, Goldbourne said he saw Thompson at about 5.30 p.m., holding a handkerchief to his eye, which was bleeding. After calling at a chemist's, where they refused to attend to the eye, Goldbourne and Thompson called at a public house at the corner of Great Crosshall Street and had a drink.

Goldbourne testified that he and Thompson were in the pub for only a few minutes. Goldbourne noticed a woman sitting behind them, who he afterwards heard was Mrs Flynn. Goldbourne said that neither he nor Thompson spoke to anyone in the pub, and they were not spoken to. Goldbourne emphatically denied that Thompson ever said to him that he had 'near kicked his wife to death'.

After Goldbourne left the box, Mr Richardson said he was unable to come to an immediate decision as to whether the accused should go for trial until he had the opportunity of going through the evidence fully. He announced he would give his decision the next afternoon.

When the court reconvened on 8 August, Mr Richardson said he had come to the conclusion that the evidence was not sufficient to place Thompson on trial on the capital charge. Thompson was then set free and left the court accompanied by friends. The police case against him had collapsed, a rare event in those days.

Poor Johnny

At about 1.30 p.m. on 5 September 1929, a stout man in a navy blue suit and wearing a khaki shirt with new black glossy boots and a dark check cap walked into Hughes Brothers pawnbrokers on Brownlow Hill. Shopman Gerard Denash was on duty at the front counter and the man said to him, 'Let's see that knife in the window', pointing to a French cook's knife. Denash directed the ruddy-faced man to another counter where John Durkin sold him the knife for 1s. 3d. About five minutes later, the man returned to the shop, saying, 'I want a razor, not more than a shilling'. Denash showed him a razor marked 9d. The man wet the back of his hand and ran the blade across it. 'That's right', he said, and bought it.

An hour and a half after the purchases of the knife and the razor, Mrs Ellen Dacey of 39 Newsham Street, on the ground floor of a tenement block off Scotland Road, heard sounds of a scuffle and raised voices coming from 39a, the flat above. Living above Mrs Dacey was her niece Mary Ellen Maguire, a mother of ten children and her husband John Maguire, a fruit seller. As Mrs Dacey listened to the commotion above her, she recognised the noise as one of the frequent quarrels between the Maguires.

However, this particular row would just not abate. Screams and shouts rang out in the afternoon quiet. Then Mrs Dacey hard Mrs Maguire call out to her 13-year-old son: 'Edward! Edward!' she cried. In Mrs Dacey's words, 'There followed the most awful screams. I was so frightened and upset that I could not leave the house'. About five minutes later more screams were heard from Mrs Maguire. 'Murder! Murder!' she shrieked.

A woman standing on her balcony in Kew Street, which overlooked the Maguire's home, heard the screams but paid little attention to what she had heard many times before. She then saw John Maguire leave the house and walk along his balcony to 33a, the home of Mrs Julia Kennedy.

Mrs Kennedy was sitting at home with her husband when Maguire shouted at the front door: 'Julia, come and see what I have done, and you Skinner [meaning Mr Kennedy], come as well'. Mrs Kennedy went into the bedroom of 39A. She saw Mrs Maguire lying on the bed with her hand up to her face. She was covered in blood and there was a large pool of blood on the floor. Julia shook Mrs Maguire and called to her: 'Ellen! Ellen!' There was no reply. A deep gash across the throat had taken her life and had nearly cut off her head.

John Maguire said he was going to give himself up and walked away from the scene along the landing in the direction of Scotland Road. A bent and bloodstained knife was found in the house. Ellen Maguire was taken to hospital but nothing could be done for her. When Mary, age 20, one of the dead woman's daughters, came home and learned of the tragedy she almost collapsed. The other children had the news broken to them by neighbours before they got home from school. Their grief was painful to see. One of the girls beat her fists on the door of the house, unable to control herself.

Eight of the children lived at home in a house of two rooms and a kitchen. Like her husband, Ellen Maguire used to hawk fruit and vegetables to supplement the family income. Her eldest son, age 23, lived in Australia and a son age 19 was at a Borstal institution for young offenders. The youngest child was 18 months old.

For several hours, crowds of mainly woman and girls stood at each end of Newsham Street, watching the arrival and departure of police cars. Constables stopped everybody who tried to go down the street, except those who had a good reason to be there.

The police did not have to search for John Maguire for long. At 7.30 a.m. the next morning he entered the main bridewell, saying, 'I want to give myself up. I am a dead man already. I should have done myself in last night. God have mercy on my soul.'

At 10 a.m. in the bridewell, John Maguire was interviewed by Detective Sergeant Bert Pritchard. He told Maguire he was going to charge him with murder. Maguire then apparently told Pritchard:

> She practically told me that the child Nellie is not mine. There are other things causing trouble all the time. She upset me yesterday and I lost my temper. I bought the knife in Brownlow Hill and I bought the razor as well.

When formally cautioned and charged at the police court, Maguire replied: 'I don't wish to say nothing'.

However, at the start of the police court proceedings on 6 September, against the advice of deputy stipendiary magistrate C. V. Addinsell, Maguire protested that he wanted to make a statement. Tears streamed down his cheeks as he talked: 'I wish to say one thing. The Lord have mercy on my wife and give her the light of heaven. There is only one thing I am very thankful for, and that is she never suffered. It was all over in a couple of minutes.'

Throughout the brief proceedings, Maguire, a thickly-set man of 43, sat in an attitude of dejection, holding his bowed head between his hands.

At the committal hearing on 18 September, Maguire, who was unrepresented, made a dramatic interruption. As his daughter Mary was giving evidence, he rose from his chair and exclaimed: 'I don't want to ask any of the witnesses any questions. Let me clear out of here and go downstairs. You can carry on all right without me.' When the magistrate pointed out that his presence could not be dispensed with, Maguire resumed his seat and listened attentively to the rest of the proceedings.

John Maguire came to trial on 8 November at St George's Hall. Leading the prosecution was P. M. Oliver MP, and Maguire's defence was in the hands of Basil Nield. After the prosecution evidence had been heard, Mr Nield sought to present a convincing defence of insanity.

Anecdotal evidence of Maguire's eccentricity came from his own relatives. None of it was likely to influence a jury but it was presented to them nevertheless. In Nield's cross-examination of young Ellen Maguire, she said her father acted 'in an abnormal way sometimes'. She said that when he returned from the war he used to go about the house with a bayonet 'as if he were at war'. Mrs Mary Hagen, Maguire's sister, said that at the age of eight he had fallen off a roof and 'Has never been right since'. The mother had always had fits and had died in a fit. An aunt, Mrs Rafferty, was in a mental ward for eighteen years.

John Maguire, a son, said his father had been 'a bit funny' since returning from the war. Two cousins of Maguire said that as a boy he would not play with other children and threw inkpots at the teacher. The war seemed to 'set him mad'.

The main witness for the defence was Dr Andrew Kefalas from Liverpool Psychotherapeutic Clinic and formerly resident medical officer at Maghull Neurological Hospital. Dr Kefalas said he had examined Maguire three times since 5 November and had concluded that he did not know what he was doing when he committed the crime. Mr Nield asked: 'Do you think, as a mental expert, that he realised the difference between right and wrong?'

Post-epileptic automatism

This is a form of epileptic seizure by which a person can undertake fairly complex acts and afterwards have no memory of them. These could be as innocuous as, for example, undressing and going to bed, or far more seriously, could be the committal of an assault or murder.

'No, I don't think he does even now,' replied the doctor.

Dr Kefalas said Maguire told him he did not care whether he was hanged or not, and that he was going back to his work. He also said Maguire was subject to buzzing in the ears, saw showers of bright sparks, went blind and dizzy, but felt well immediately afterwards. That, said the doctor, was typical of an attack of petit mal. He was of the opinion that Maguire committed the crime in a state of post-epileptic automatism. He did not know he was attacking his wife, though he might have thought at one moment that he was attacking something.

The doctor's evidence was severely dented when, in answer to the judge, he said that Maguire was not, in his opinion, in a state of automatism when he bought the knife and razor, nor when he went and told the neighbours what he had done. Maguire, in Kefalas's opinion, suffered from minor epilepsy and was also a dipsomaniac.

The crown's medical witness was Dr Ahern of Walton Prison. He said he could find no evidence of mental unsoundness nor of any form of epilepsy. In cross examination Dr Ahern said Maguire told him of dreams he had had some months before. Maguire had said: 'You may think I am mad, but I saw a devil at the foot of the bed in the air. Seven devils must have got hold of me when I did this lot.' Dr Ahern did not think Maguire was pretending, but he attributed the visions to alcoholism.

Throughout the trial, Maguire sat in the dock with his head in his hands. Only when a witness was called upon to recognise him did he raise his head. The jury, which included two women, took half an hour to return a verdict of guilty. Maguire stood firmly at the rail of the dock while Mr Justice Humphreys passed sentence of death. Then Maguire asked if he might say a few words. The judge nodded and in a clear voice Maguire declared:

> Before I go I wish to thank from the bottom of my heart counsel who defended me, and the medical representative who spoke on my behalf. I hope that before long they both will be at the top of the ladder. As regards the other witnesses . . .

Here the judge interposed: 'I cannot listen to speeches now. Go down.' Maguire stepped down briskly and unconcernedly, sobs were heard and then the screams of a woman crying 'Poor Johnny!' The woman, Maguire's sister Mary Hagen, had to be helped from the hall. Several of the Maguire children had waited in the room for the verdict. They had to be led away, crying bitterly.

John Maguire was executed at Walton at 8 a.m. on Tuesday 26 November 1929. An hour before the appointed time, people began to gather in the half light of dawn outside the prison entrance. Almost first to arrive was a group of shawl-clad women from the Newsham Street neighbourhood. Several carried infants wrapped in their shawls and others had young children clinging to their skirts. They all wore clean white aprons.

As 8 o'clock drew near, the crowd swelled until there were over 250 present, the majority being men who had stopped for a few minutes before going to work. Several of the women had been weeping before

they arrived at the prison and they seemed to be keeping back the tears with difficulty.

As soon as the stroke of eight rang out from the prison clock, all the women knelt on the wet roadway and bowed their heads in prayer. As the hour slowly rang, the women prayed aloud. There was a moment or two of silence until a further note sounded inside the prison, and then hats were donned and the kneeling women slowly rose to their feet. Another gong sounded, and there was a frantic rush to the prison gate to await the posting of the usual notice.

When the crowd had settled and were speaking in subdued tones, a shriek of anguish startled them. 'Oh Johnny, my lovely brother, my poor Johnny!', screamed a woman. The crowd made way for a woman of stout build as she fought her way through the throng with tears streaming down her face. 'Oh Johnny!' she cried continually. 'They have taken my poor dear brother!' When she reached the massive gates of the prison she flung herself to her knees and screamed again: 'Oh Johnny, come back to me! Johnny! Johnny!' Several neighbours tried to comfort her, but she shook them off. The distracted woman was Mrs Mary Hagen of Back Queen Anne Street, eldest sister of Maguire, who had created a scene in the assize court. Her daughter then tried to pull her mother away, shouting: 'Oh my mother, my mother, come home!'

Eventually, four policemen managed to half drag and half carry the unfortunate woman away. She was now screaming and kicking violently. Just as they carried her to the middle of the road, a taxicab drew up with a woman driver. She was immediately recognised by some of Mrs Hagan's companions and offered to drive the woman home. As Mrs Hagan was helped in to the taxi, she recovered a little and sobbed: 'I never said goodbye properly to poor Johnny. He's gone, we'll never ever see him again.'

The official notices, which were posted on the prison gate at about 8.10 a.m. were as follows:

> Declaration of the Sheriff – We, the undersigned, hereby declare that the judgement of death was this day executed on John Maguire, in his Majesty's Prison, Liverpool, in our presence, Dated this 26th day of November 1929 – Geoffrey H. Wright, Under-Sheriff of Lancaster, Justice of the Peace; Charles F. Rich, Governor; John Irving Lane, R.C. Chaplain of the Prison.

> Certificate of the Surgeon – I, John Maurice Ahern, surgeon of H. M. Prison Liverpool, hereby certify that I, this day, examined the body of John Maguire on whom judgement of death was this day executed in the said prison, and that on examination, the said John Maguire was dead. [Dated and signed] J. M. Ahern.'

It was understood that a newly erected scaffold was used for the first time that morning. The executioner was Tom Pierrepoint, assisted by T. M. Phillips. The allowed drop was 7 feet 10 inches.

More local titles from
Carnegie Publishing
&
Palatine Books . . .

to order contact
Booksource
tel: 0845 370 0063

Murder in Edwardian Merseyside
David Parry

Liverpool at the end of the Victorian era was still a place of poverty, slum housing and hardship. Forced to endure appalling living conditions, many turned to drink and violence, the one often born out of the other.

The 43 murders recounted in this fascinating book range from the downright evil to the heartbreakingly sad, and the ways in which they were dealt with by the police and courts of the time are both interesting and revealing.

A great piece of social history with additional material on issues such as hanging, infanticide, drunkenness, unemployment and religion.

Palatine   softback   128 pages   ISBN 10: 1-874181-27-6   ISBN 13: 978-1-874181-27-9   **£7.95**

Growin' Up
One Scouser's social history
Johnnie Woods

Johnnie Woods had a rare talent as a writer. He avoids both the rose-tinted nostalgia and the bitterness that are typical of many books which deal with the Great Depression and the Second World War. With a humour and an honesty that are most revealing, he paints a picture of his Liverpool during those hard times; a picture that is realistic, down to earth, and immensely entertaining.

He pays warm tribute to 'the guts, the rough dignity and the tenacity' of ordinary folk and gives an incredibly vivid impression of life for a youngster in one of the 'rougher' districts of the city.

A hugely enjoyable book that will appeal to Liverpudlians of all ages.

Palatine   softback   96 pages   ISBN 10: 1-874181-23-3   ISBN 13: 978-1-874181-23-1   **£5.95**

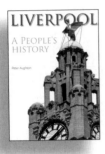

Liverpool: a people's history
Peter Aughton

Liverpool: A people's history is the best-selling book about this great city, from its foundation in 1207 to European Capital of Culture 801 years later. Beautifully illustrated and accessibly written, this is by far the best introduction to Liverpool: a great way to understand and appreciate this remarkable city.

'*... a fascinating insight into a great and unique city and its people*' Liverpool Echo

Carnegie	356 pages	over 200 illustrations, mostly in full colour		June 2007
hardback		ISBN 10: 1-85936-161-7	ISBN 13: 978-1-85936-161-0	**£20.00**
softback		ISBN 10: 1-85936-168-4	ISBN 13: 978-1-85936-168-9	**£14.95**

A small Tudor town
Liverpool in the sixteenth century
Janet Hollinshead

Tudor Liverpool was a small place, typical of many towns, yet already showing some early signs of later greatness. A fascinating new book on the city's early history.

Carnegie	softback	176 pages	ISBN 10: 1-85936-149-8	ISBN 13: 978-1-85936-149-8	**£13.99**

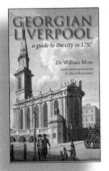

Georgian Liverpool
Dr William Moss

Dr William Moss wrote a detailed guide book to the city to allow them fully to understand and appreciate the sights of the town. The second edition of this wonderful guide is reproduced here and provides a truly fascinating window on Liverpool's past.

Palatine	softback	208 pages	ISBN 978-1-874181-46-0	**£7.95**

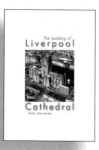

The Building of Liverpool Cathedral

Peter Kennerley

Brilliant account of the building of this magnificent place of worship, and the creation of a cathedral community in a great city.

| hardback (limited edition) | ISBN 10: 1-85936-108-0 | £30.00 |
| softback | ISBN 13: 978-1-85936-173-3 | £10.00 |

Frederick William Dwelly
First dean of Liverpool, 1881–1957

Peter Kennerley

Peter Kennerley was Education Officer at Liverpool Cathedral, during which time he was able to research and write this biography of Dean Dwelly.

Carnegie   hardback   304 pages   ISBN 10: 1-85936-133-1   ISBN 13: 978-1-85936-133-7   **£20.00**

Life, love and washing up
The musings of a Liverpool columnist

David Charters

Musings on life, often funny and sometimes sad, all highly entertaining.

'David's delight in the English language and his insights ... illuminate this splendid book.'

Palatine   softback   112 pages   ISBN 10: 1-874181-38-1   ISBN 13: 978-1-874181-38-5   **£4.95**

The Leeds and Liverpool Canal
A history and guide
Mike Clarke

No one could be better qualified than Mike Clarke to describe this, the longest and arguably most successful of all British canals. A fully illustrated history.

Carnegie   softback   288 pages   ISBN 10: 1-85936-013-0   ISBN 13: 978-1-85936-013-2   **£12.00**

The Lancashire witch-craze
Jennet Preston and the Lancashire Witches, 1612
Jonathan Lumby

The author presents many new insights, and by placing the events in their wider European context explains them more satisfactorily than ever before.

Carnegie   softback   224 pages   ISBN 10: 1-85936-025-4   ISBN 13: 978-1-85936-025-5   **£7.50**

Wonderfull Discoverie of Witches in the Countie of Lancaster
A reproduction of Thomas Potts' original 1612 book

Nearly 400 years after they were tried, there is still huge interest in the Lancashire Witches. Their activities, arrest and trials have been the subject of many books, none of which could have been written without reference to Thomas Potts' original book, reproduced here from the original. Essential reading for all those with an interest in the subject.

Carnegie   softback   224 pages   ISBN 10: 1-85936-100-5   ISBN 13: 978-1-85936-100-9   **£6.95**

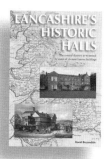

Lancashire's historic halls
The county's history as witnessed by some of its most famous buildings
David Brazendale

The ancient halls of Lancashire are of national significance: remarkable as an architectural type and of huge importance within their neighbourhoods. David Brazendale explores each with reference to its wider importance in the county's history: he explores witchcraft through Samlesbury; the Renaissance through Towneley Hall; and so on. A great read.

Carnegie   softback   288 pages   ISBN 10: 1-85936-106-4   ISBN 13: 978-1-85936-106-1   **£10.00**

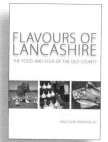

Flavours of Lancashire
The food and folk of the old county
Malcolm Greenhalgh

A lively, beautifully produced and illustrated celebration of Lancashire's rich and colourful food heritage. With recipes, social history and much more.

Palatine   softback   160 pages   ISBN 10: 1-874181-39-X   ISBN 13: 978-1-874181-39-2   **£10.00**

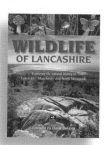

Wildlife of Lancashire
Exploring the natural history of Lancashire, Manchester and North Merseyside
Foreword by David Bellamy

Full colour throughout, this sumptuous book covers most of the old county.

Carnegie   hardback   352 pages   ISBN 10: 1-85936-118-8   ISBN 13: 978-1-85936-118-4   **£20.00**